Kat doesn't just write words, she speaks tru
decade and seen her live out every chapter o
and real-life experience, her words will give you tools and equip you to dive into your own story and seek the heart of God when it comes to relationships.

BIANCA JUAREZ OLTHOFF, speaker, pastor, and bestselling author of *How to Have Your Life Not Suck*

In our sex-saturated culture, Christians constantly seek how to respond in both a compelling and compassionate way. Kat has done just that. *Sexless in the City* does a fantastic job of weaving together personal narrative with biblical truth and doesn't shrink away from the hard questions people really want answered. You may not agree with everything in here, but you will be better for examining faith and sex through a holistic and biblical lens.

JON TYSON, lead pastor of Church of the City New York, author of *Beautiful Resistance*

I know what it's like to hide and crush my sexuality in the name of purity culture. I know what it's like to see my self-image, my body, be warped and hindered by old ways of thinking. Harris invites us into an expansive, generous, biblical view of intimacy that is so needed. I wish I'd had this book when I was younger. But I'm glad we have it now.

JEDIDIAH JENKINS, *New York Times* bestselling author of *To Shake the Sleeping Self* and *Like Streams to the Ocean*

Kat is sincere in her deep love for Christ and her desire to biblically wrestle with her questions around sex, sexuality, desire, singleness, femininity, relationships, and the way of Jesus. This book is vulnerable, biblically sound, and fastened tightly to the promises of God. It's a book where sexual brokenness doesn't get to have the final say. Instead, as you journey through its pages, you may just find freedom, healing, and restoration with our amazing God.

ANDI ANDREW, author, speaker, and church planter

Kat Harris has written an incredibly insightful, bold, and challenging body of work in *Sexless in the City*. It is a genuine road map we can all follow to help lead us in discovering some of the answers to questions, concerns, and thoughts most people are afraid to talk about.

> **TIM TIMBERLAKE**, lead pastor of Celebration Church, author of *The Power of 1440* and *Abandon*

This is such an important discussion, and I am so thankful for the deep dive this book takes us on to educate us with truth on God's intent for sexuality, roles, boundaries, purity, and the simultaneous struggle and joy it all can bring. This is a must-read!

> **LAUREN SCRUGGS KENNEDY**, *New York Times* bestselling author of *Your Beautiful Heart* and *Still LoLo*, lifestyle and wellness entrepreneur

Christians are notoriously bad at talking about sex. *Sexless in the City* is a layered and nuanced conversation around singleness and sex, dating and desire that people of faith need far more than they realize. Kat Harris shares her own journey with remarkable vulnerability—sparing no detail and granting no respect to cultural taboos—to invite readers to confront their own hidden struggles and fears. Remarkably, this book normalizes healthy discussion about sexuality without abandoning faith as irrelevant or dismissing the sacred Scriptures as antiquated. I recommend this book, but only for brave believers who are ready to be transformed by the renewing of their minds.

> **JONATHAN MERRITT**, contributing writer for *The Atlantic*, author of *Learning to Speak God from Scratch*

Raised in the stifling narratives of both purity and hook-up cultures, Kat Harris reminds us we needn't pick a side: pure or impure, virgin or whore. With honest retellings of Bible stories, Kat presents an ever-loving God who desires his women embodied, aligned, and genuinely free. Away with the church's vague pleasantries and unhappily-ever-afters; *Sexless in the City* offers a sacred sexual ethic that will actually work.

> **BRENDA MARIE DAVIES**, author of *On Her Knees: Memoir of a Prayerful Jezebel*

Throughout these words, Kat invites us on her personal journey of trusting God's design for sex in her life. She's honest, vulnerable, and relatable in the ways she has grown and been stretched in believing what God's Word says about sex for the single girl.

JAMIE IVEY, bestselling author, podcast host

Shout-out to Kat for tackling one of the most hidden and lied about topics in the church and beyond. From biblical truth to wild and fun stories, there's no better read on moving from a life of secrecy to fully coming into our godly sexuality. Buy this book, read it intently, and get out of the dark about how God intentionally created us all.

TONI COLLIER, founder of Broken Crayons,
colead pastor of Hillsong Atlanta

Kat uncovers deep insight on topics more commonly swept under the rug or discussed only in whispers or shouts. This is what it looks like to be a woman who follows God, but does so shame-free. Let the light shine with clarity on the truth we all have missed along the way so that we can celebrate being whole, as we are, in the way God made us.

JENNA KUTCHER, host of the
Goal Digger podcast

Kat is the voice of Christ-following women who believe there is more out there to who we are than what we've been taught. Kat has the courage to ask tough questions that so many feel too afraid or embarrassed to ask. Kat's vulnerability and openness about her own journey help sweep away the pervasive shame about our bodies, sex, and pleasure and replace it with insight and empowerment about who God created us to be as human beings. Her words, wisdom, and biblical knowledge help set women free.

DR. THERESE MASCARDO, licensed clinical
psychologist, founder of Exploring Therapy

Kat Harris honestly, and sometimes humorously, addresses issues that were wholly neglected by faith mentors and, dare I say, our own mothers. As Harris questions the shameful narrative many learned in their youth, she paints a new picture, one laced with grace and restoration. This book will prove to be an invaluable road map for women as they navigate their sexuality in this day and age.

TIFFANY BLUHM, author of *Prey Tell*,
cohost of the *Why Tho* podcast

At last! This is the book I wish I had when I was a young woman weighed down by shame about my sexual desire. These are the words I needed when I thought I'd be condemned forevermore. Kat gracefully undoes harmful purity culture narratives and replaces them with rooted biblical truth about the beauty of our sexual design. This is a beautiful, brave must-read!

KAIT WARMAN, author, dating coach,
and founder of Heart of Dating

Women are hungry for truth. We need a space where we are free to ask the hard questions about romance, sexuality and the Bible, where the longing in our soul and the questions in our hearts can be heard, and answered. Whether you are married or single, Christian or not, this book packs a punch in practical takeaways and applicable wisdom.

ASHLEY ABERCROMBIE, author of *Rise of the Truth Teller* and *Love Is the Resistance*

Kat Harris is the vulnerable and bold voice you want to hear when it comes to unpacking single sexuality. She validates the confusing parts of finding a sexual ethic and then gives you a road map for finding your own. An excellent read!

CELESTE HOLBROOK, PhD, sex educator

SEXLESS
in the city

SEXLESS *in the city*

A SOMETIMES SASSY, SOMETIMES PAINFUL, ALWAYS HONEST LOOK AT DATING, DESIRE, AND SEX

KAT HARRIS

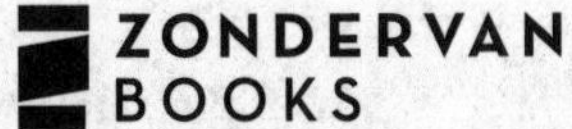

ZONDERVAN BOOKS

Sexless in the City

Requests for information should be addressed to:
Zondervan, *3900 Sparks Dr. SE, Grand Rapids, Michigan 49546*

Zondervan titles may be purchased in bulk for educational, business, fundraising, or sales promotional use. For information, please email SpecialMarkets@Zondervan.com.

ISBN 978-0-310-36105-3 (audio)

Library of Congress Cataloging-in-Publication Data

Names: Harris, Kat, 1985- author.
Title: Sexless in the city : a sometimes sassy, sometimes painful, always honest look at dating, desire, and sex / Kat Harris.
Description: Grand Rapids : Zondervan, 2021. | Includes bibliographical references. | Summary: "Navigating singleness as a woman of faith can be a struggle fest, but it doesn't have to be. In Sexless in the City, podcaster, founder of The Refined Woman, and Texan turned New Yorker Kat Harris shares her messy, honest, and unlikely journey to discovering God's heart for singleness, sexuality, desire, and our purpose within it all"— Provided by publisher.
Identifiers: LCCN 2020048212 (print) | LCCN 2020048213 (ebook) | ISBN 9780310361039 (trade paperback) | ISBN 9780310361046 (ebook)
Subjects: LCSH: Christian women—Conduct of life. | Christian women—Sexual behavior. | Christian women—Religious life.
Classification: LCC BV4527 .H38549 2021 (print) | LCC BV4527 (ebook) | DDC 248.8/43—dc23
LC record available at https://lccn.loc.gov/2020048212
LC ebook record available at https://lccn.loc.gov/2020048213

The names and identifying details of some individuals have been changed to protect their privacy.

Author is represented by The Christopher Ferebee Agency, www.christopherferebee.com.

Cover design: Lindy Martin / Faceout Studio
Cover illustrations: Shutterstock; Stocksy
Interior design: Kait Lamphere

Printed in the United States of America

---

21 22 23 24 25 26 27 28 29 30 31 /LSC/ 14 13 12 11 10 9 8 7 6 5 4 3 2 1

Gaw-Gaw,
you trailblazing, faithful, fiery, feisty,
glitter-wearing, cheesecake-lovin' woman,
I love you forever

Writing for me feels like getting naked in public. . . . When I finally get up the guts to crack through the ice of my mind, I find myself in an odd universe of feelings I didn't know I felt, and memories I didn't know I carried.

—*Shauna Niequist*

CONTENTS

PHASE 3: THE PRACTICAL

INTRODUCTION

> They had come to the end of the pavement, to the end of the streetlights. The road under their feet was slippery with spring mud, and the grass that brushed against their legs was wet with dew.
> Abra asked, "Where are we going?"
> —*John Steinbeck*

I grew up in Southern Christian culture in the early 2000s during the height of what's known as the purity movement. Even though I didn't grow up in a Christian home per se, I did grow up in the suburbs of Texas, aka the buckle of the Bible Belt. Long before I ever knew anything about inviting Jesus into my heart, Christian culture was the air I breathed. Like millions of other angsty teens during the whole purity movement, I was taught to save sex for marriage because it was God's best, and given a strict set of dating rules in order to maintain my sexual purity. I'm not sure the words were ever spoken out loud, but the message I internalized was this: my salvation seemed somehow dependent on what I did or didn't do between my legs.[1] With such high stakes, my physical experiences with guys vacillated between being nonexistent and consisting of brief moments of passion laced with shame and regret.

Fast-forward a few decades, and we are living in a time when sexual scandal in the American evangelical church is widely being exposed, and rightfully so. It turns out many of the male pastors preaching sexual purity from the pulpit were the ones secretly addicted to porn and running around on their wives; it's devastating, disorienting, and completely unacceptable. The brokenness is as deep as it is wide. I have dear friends who have been so hurt by the sexual narratives offered by the church and the hypocrisy of its leaders that they've left the faith altogether. To be honest, I don't blame them. Reducing a relationship with God to a set of rules to earn our seat at the table diminishes the grace, vision, and power of the gospel. This view is terribly broken. The church has really blown it.

Amid a painfully awkward and messy Christian dating culture, navigating my own sexual desire has felt both lonely and wildly confusing. At times, part of me was proud for holding on to my virginity when many of my friends had *fallen off the bandwagon*, while the other part of me felt shame at my total lack of experience.

I was sick of hearing mostly male pastors teach about waiting until marriage to have sex and doing it "God's way" when most of them got married in their early twenties and had no idea what it was like to actually abstain from sex for decades. I was even more sick of many male pastors telling me to live a life of purity when behind closed doors they themselves weren't. It's not that what they were saying wasn't necessarily true; it's just the former had no idea what it was really like to date and be single in today's culture, and the latter had no integrity. And to be frank, I wanted to hear from someone who was actually single, in her thirties or beyond, walking the walk.

I was tired of pumping the brakes in the heat of the moment. I was tired of negotiating my physical boundaries and feeling guilt and shame when I messed up. But mostly, I was just tired of keeping my pants on. I was quickly approaching thirty years old, and I felt like a sexual infant.[2] I was over it.

A few years ago, I got dumped. I was as lost as I was hurt and heartbroken, and I finally hit my breaking point.

***

In the fifteenth century, a Japanese military commander broke one of his favorite Chinese tea bowls. He sent it out for repair, and it returned bound together with metal staples in an attempt to mask its fractures. The commander hated it and demanded that his team try again. There had to be a better way.

In a moment of inspiration, one of the artists created a glue infused with the finest gold powder. In a painstakingly slow process, the artist reconstructed every single broken piece and jagged edge of that bowl with the golden glue. This time, instead of hiding the brokenness, the gold highlighted every crack and crevice of the bowl's shattered past. The final product was exquisite. The commander loved it, and the restored bowl became one of his most prized possessions.

This concept became known as *kintsugi*, or literally "to join with gold."[3] The goal wasn't perfection but bringing honor and value through a process of meticulous restoration of that which has been broken.

***

I believe God wants to weave gold into the fractured areas of our lives, specifically the shame-filled narratives that purity culture gave so many of us. I believe God wants to restore that brokenness into something more beautiful than we could ever imagine. Somehow, my breaking became an access point to stepping into untapped freedom and restoration with God, myself, and the world around me. And it was in the reconstructing, the piecing back together of my heart and story, that I began to find my way. A new way.

The commander's artist understood something all those years ago: brokenness doesn't have the final word. In fact, while the tea bowl may have started out valuable, it was only after its reconstruction that it became priceless. But first it had to break.

This is my *kintsugi* story.

PHASE ONE

The Deconstruction

Chapter One

MY BREAKING POINT

Life in Lubbock, Texas, taught me two things: One is that God loves you and you're going to burn in hell. The other is that sex is the most awful, filthy thing on earth, and you should save it for someone you love.

—*Butch Hancock*

Not having sex was easy. That was mostly because from my teens through midtwenties, my dating life was about as exciting as staring at a blank wall. Still, I was pretty high and mighty about the whole virginity thing. One time I even stopped being friends with an old roommate because she started having sex with her boyfriend.

All of that changed when I moved to New York City at twenty-seven, in hopes of becoming the next big fashion photographer. My first year living in the city, I went on more dates than I had in the previous decade. This isn't saying much since I went almost seven years postcollege without going on a single date. Nonetheless, I was dating regularly, and it was a foreign experience. As it turns out, it's a lot harder not to have sex when you're actually going on dates.

In the midst of this, on a random fall Friday night at a friend's dinner party, I met him. It was like hearing a song for the first time and within the first few notes not really understanding the why or how but just knowing you're going to love that song. I was a goner.

Add to that scenario a few glasses of wine, a makeout on a Brooklyn street corner that felt straight out of a movie, and did I mention he was wearing a leather jacket? Yeah, my resolve was about as strong as a wet paper towel trying to hold up a fifty-pound dumbbell. I found myself hopping into a cab back to his place, and my thirtyish-year commitment to abstain from sex until marriage almost flew out the window as fast as my shirt came off.

In the wee hours of the morning, I tiptoed through his apartment, searching for my strewn-about clothes. If I left before the sun was fully out, and we didn't technically have sex, then I hadn't done anything wrong. Right?

On my sunrise cab ride back to Brooklyn, I was still intoxicated with all the feels from the night before (and probably a little wine too). I had never gone home with a guy in my entire life. In the past, I always felt guilty if I even got close to going past my physical boundaries. But for some reason when I blazed right past them this time, I didn't, and that surprised me. After years of being on my virgin high horse, I wasn't ready to confront how weak my conviction was when actually given the opportunity to abstain. Not yet anyway. I wanted a little more time on cloud nine before I started to think about how we were going to move forward since on night one we had everything but sex.

Overnight, my virginity was hanging on by a lacy thread.

GOING ALL THE WAY

This guy pursued me, planned romantic dates, and texted me throughout the day when he was thinking of me. For the first time in a long time, I felt like a woman. He was honest and vulnerable with his feelings for me, a far cry from what I had experienced in the past. We were *that* couple, always making out in the middle of a restaurant while our waiter was trying to take our order. I was like Will Ferrell in the movie *Elf*, barging into his dad's office, throwing off his hat, and shouting, "I'm in love, I'm in love, and I don't care who knows it."[1] I was smitten, and I didn't care how annoying we were.

As the days and weeks passed, I started to wonder* why I was waiting until marriage to have sex. In the heat of the moment, "because the Bible told me so" no longer felt like a compelling reason to keep my pants on. And even though I graduated college with a Bible degree, for the life of me I couldn't tell you one verse that said, "Don't have sex until marriage." Was it some antiquated Christian norm that was no longer relevant?

As I looked around, I noticed that a lot of Christians I knew were having sex and even living with their boyfriends. It was all pretty hush-hush. But just because no one wants to talk about something doesn't mean it's not a thing. Christian or not, I felt like I might be the only virgin left in New York City.

I was so conflicted, but at the end of the day, something still stopped me every time from going all the way with him.

A few months down the road, I was in the city for back-to-back meetings and swung by his place for a quick hello on my way to yoga. He opened the door, and I immediately felt an invisible wall between us. He cut to the chase. Turns out, as it had always been a deal breaker for me to have sex before marriage, it was a deal breaker for him not to. With me in a gridlock of confusion, we were at an impasse. So, just like that, we broke up. As quickly as we fell into a relationship, we fell out. Choking back tears, I grabbed my yoga mat and left.

---

* Yes, this is 100 percent a nod to Carrie Bradshaw from *Sex in the City*. Sorry, I couldn't help myself.

Here's the thing about heartbreak: in a breath you go from being blissfully happy to feeling like someone threw a bag of bricks on your back. As I rode the jam-packed subway car uptown to class, quiet tears slid down my cheeks. I was heartbroken.

CHASING THE PAIN

Have you ever tried to tear a piece of paper in a clean line? Inevitably you lose control of the tear, and it ends up all jagged and uneven. Then you wonder why you didn't go into the other room and grab the scissors from the junk drawer in the first place. It would've taken all of two seconds. That's what our breakup was like.

We tried the "let's just be friends" scenario. As with most things, it worked until it didn't. One night we were cooking dinner, listening to music, dancing in the kitchen—you know, things you do with someone who's *just* a friend. I can't remember how or when, but at some point, we crossed the invisible line we had been tiptoeing around for months. We kissed, and our bodies didn't skip a beat. Things went from zero to sixty, and within minutes we approached our all-too-familiar impasse. I wanted to have sex with him—my body and my heart ached for it—but something still stopped me. It was our final breaking point.

This time it was over for real.

In the months after our breakup, I was in a fog. Chasing the pain away, I went to bars, danced on tables, got drunk, made out with strangers, and even took some home with me. I dated guys who were emotionally unavailable and going nowhere fast. I tried to convince myself I was just having my "single ladies" moment in New York City, living it up like the rest of them. And to be honest, I did have some fun times. But inside, heartbroken and disoriented, I was a mess.

A FORK IN THE ROAD

It was one thing to be sixteen years old in youth group and make a promise to God that I wouldn't have sex until I was married. But I was almost thirty, for crying out loud, with no prospects in sight. Even though I grew up in an outspoken purity culture, the church now seemed all but silent on the topic. This no sex thing was weighing me down, and I was ready for liberation.

Like any rational person wanting to justify a decision, I went to the person in my life I thought would agree with me: my best friend. She wasn't a Christian and didn't believe in saving sex for marriage. If there was anyone who would be on board with my new decision, it would be her.

One night while we were doing laundry together at her Brooklyn apartment, I casually brought up how I was considering having sex in my dating relationships moving forward. She slowly put down the T-shirt she was folding, looked me square in the eye, and said, "No way." My head cocked to the side like a confused puppy, and my eyes blinked a few times, trying to bring into focus what she had just said.

She went on to say she wanted me to have sex so I could get on with my life. But she knew sex meant something different to me, that my relationship with God really mattered to me, and there must be some good reason why for almost thirty years I had chosen not to have sex. She challenged me to figure out what I believed about sex and God and why. She told me to read my Bible and pray. She pointed me to the Jesus she didn't even believe in and made it clear that until I did some real soul searching, she wasn't going to support my newfound determination to have sex.

This was the last thing I expected to come out of her mouth. I was as shocked as I was annoyed by her response. She didn't agree with my conviction, but she was unwilling to see me compromise my beliefs because I was tired of them. She called me out in the most loving of ways and fought for me when I didn't feel like being fought for.

Now that is a good friend.

I was at a fork in the road. Option one: ignore her, go to someone else who would agree with me, and do what I set out to do. Option two: pause, take inventory, commit to the tedious work of self-examination, dig deep into my own heart, seek God, and ask the hard questions. Much to my own surprise, I found myself taking the latter. She was right; I needed to figure out what God and the Bible said about it all, and then I needed to decide if I cared about what it had to say.

What I thought would be a few hours of quiet time with God turned into a multiyear journey of searching for answers to my biggest questions about sex, sexuality, desire, singleness, femininity, relationships, and the ways of Jesus. I started by looking up every single verse in the Bible that talked about sex. Turns out God has a lot to say about not only sex but also desire, passion, gender roles, and the collision of our bodies and spirits.

I read dozens of books about sex by scientists to psychologists to Jewish feminists.[2] Like a journalist hungry for a story, I asked questions to anyone who would give me their ear, from pastors to strangers at bars. I became that girl you regretted starting a conversation with at a party.*

I thought I'd walk away from this little journey confident in my decision to have sex in my dating relationships. I couldn't have been more wrong.

---

* Search YouTube for the *SNL* sketch "The Girl You Wish You Wouldn't Have Started a Conversation With at a Party." Yeah, I was that girl.

A HEADS-UP

Just as my story was and is not linear, it may at times feel like I'm all over the place. But each word, page, and story is purposeful. You're going to have to trust me. I promise to remain rooted in Scripture, share my story as truthfully as possible, and land the plane so you can walk away from this book equipped with a biblical vision for dating, desire, and sex and with the tools to develop a healthy sexual ethic with clarity, vision, and freedom from fear and shame. With that said, I have created a framework to empower you to navigate your theology and beliefs surrounding sexuality from a holistic place. I've done this by separating this book into three distinct phases.

PHASE 1: THE DECONSTRUCTION

To move forward, we first have to look backward. And we have to be honest. We'll walk through questions like:

- What do you believe about sex, your body, and sexuality, and why?
- How did these beliefs come about?
- Which of these beliefs are true, and which are rooted in fear and shame?

The goal of phase 1 is to identify and dismantle beliefs that are out of alignment with Scripture and the heart of God.

We currently live in a culture where the deconstruction phase can easily turn into a lifestyle. So much disillusionment can rise to the surface in this process that it can make you want to either walk away from everything for good or just sit in the deconstruction indefinitely. That's not what I want for you. My heart is to create the space you need to reconstruct your theology and beliefs on a firm foundation.[3] The psalmist says, "Unless the LORD builds the house, the builders labor in vain."[4] I hit my breaking point all those years ago because my theology on sex and sexuality was based on a set of rules with little to no biblical context or vision. I built a house of cards, and as soon as a gust of wind came through, it collapsed to the ground. I don't know about you, but I don't want to build another house in vain. The writer of Proverbs says, "The wise in heart are called discerning, and gracious words promote instruction."[5] I too desire a deep discernment for you that leads to practical application in your life, a wisdom that will guide you to our next phase.

PHASE 2: THE RECONSTRUCTION

Phase 2 is about rebuilding a firm foundation of sexual narratives and beliefs rooted in biblical teaching. This is also where I'll cast a renewed biblical vision for sexuality, desire, identity, and intimacy. We'll walk through what our core identity is as humans made in the image of God, and I'll answer questions like:

- How does the way of Jesus differ from what popular culture and the church offer in regard to our identity and sexuality?
- From Old Testament to New, what does the Bible really say about sex and sexuality?
- What is God's vision for relationships and intimacy?
- What does the Bible really say about sex outside of marriage, if anything?

PHASE 3: THE PRACTICAL

Head knowledge and theology only get us so far. This is why we need phase 3: the practical. This final section is all about merging what we've learned with our daily lives, because true transformation happens when knowledge collides with our experience. The practical makes sense only in context of phases 1 and 2. In this section I'll cover topics like:

- How to holistically embrace your sexuality.
- How to establish physical boundaries in dating.
- How to pursue wholeness before pursuing a relationship.
- How to take the awkward out of dating.

My aim throughout all this isn't to tell you what to do but to equip you with the tools to dig into your own story and seek the heart of God on your own accord. Take your time. This process requires work, work I can't do for you. But it will be work you'll be so glad you did. Trust me.

Now, let me clarify a few things. Throughout these pages, I'm not speaking on behalf of all people for all time. I grew up in the South in the '90s and early 2000s and will be speaking from personal experience. I also want to acknowledge that I am a white heterosexual cisgender woman who grew up primarily in the upper middle class. I can't deny the immense privilege I have experienced because of those two things.

I am no expert, philosopher, or anthropologist either. I'm simply a girl who grew up in Southern evangelical church culture and who has had experiences (positive and negative) that led her down the path of asking why. All I can do is speak to my experience with humility and honesty. I ask that you be gracious with me, open, and curious. Whether or not you agree with me, my hope is that all of this encourages you to pause, think, question, and do your own soul searching.

This book is not a theological manifesto, nor is it gospel truth. I am not God. I've been wrong before, and chances are I'll be wrong again. It's also not an argument proving why you should or shouldn't have sex. It's not a set of rules either—I think we have about enough of those, don't you? It's not a script to regurgitate to the person you're dating about what you believe about sex. And it's definitely not a ten-step guide to meeting your husband. Much to my dismay, there's no formula for that either.

However, it is my story, the story I wish I had years ago when I felt terrified of sex, desire, dating, and relationships. I want to be the voice for you that I didn't have, if you'll let me. The voice of a woman in today's culture who loves God, is walking the path of singleness, hopeful for a relationship, connected to her sexual desire in a holistic way, and not preaching a message I haven't walked. I didn't meet my person and get married in my early twenties. I have online dated. I have been ghosted. I have fumbled my way through this journey . . . and I'm still on it. This isn't just theory or theology for me; it's my life.

My hope as we walk through these pages together is that my imperfect, doubt-filled story, full of fumbles, failures, hard questions, and everything in between, will show you first that you are not alone in your experience and second that you have permission to examine the narratives you were given and to ask hard questions.

What I know is this: God is not threatened by your questions or doubts. If God is real, and I believe He is, He's not that insecure. Even though the gray spaces of our lives can feel scary to us, God isn't afraid of them. He has the grace and patience to walk with us as we pursue wholeness and search for truth. My prayer is that God will speak to you in unique ways as you dive into my story and that where there is confusion, God will bring clarity, and where there is shame, God's healing waters will wash over you, bringing unbelievable freedom. And ultimately, that God will show you His loving, gracious, restorative, and safe heart.

All right, let's do this.

TAKE IT FURTHER

1. What did you learn about sex from your parents, school, peers, and any sort of church or religious institutions you were affiliated with?
2. Up until this point, what are the beliefs you have held about dating, desire, and sex? When and why did you start adhering to these beliefs?
3. What do you hope to learn throughout this book?

Chapter Two

MODEST IS HOTTEST

REFRAMING SEXUAL RESPONSIBILITY

> We teach girls to shrink themselves, to make themselves smaller. We say to girls, you can have ambition, but not too much. You should aim to be successful, but not too successful. Otherwise, you would threaten the man.
>
> —*Chimamanda Ngozi Adichie*

In college I was a counselor at a Christian sports camp for rich high school kids. After finals ended, I'd pack my bags and make the eight-hour drive to camp. It was in the middle of nowhere and a complete break from everyday life. No computers or cell phones were allowed unless you left camp grounds for a night off. There weren't even mirrors in the cabins. And there were cheers for everything; it was like being in a constant flash mob. All day long, out of nowhere, people would bust into a chorus of cheers and choreography. My first week of training was overwhelming, but by the time the campers showed up, I knew every word to every single one of those cheers. High school students would drive in from all over the United States, with car windows painted and trunks filled to the brim for every sort of costume party imaginable, to stay at camp for an entire month. I could hardly wrap my mind around the whole thing.

All summer long it was approximately a thousand degrees outside with 99 percent humidity. From one-piece bathing suits before they were cool (meaning they were about as flattering as a wet suit) to oversized T-shirts and baggy long shorts, the dress code for us girls was less than ideal. They may as well have given us burlap sacks to wear. I looked like a blob and was a tornado of sweat and BO. You could smell me coming from a mile away. I've honestly never felt less attractive.

The guys, however, would prance into lunch shirtless, with sunscreen and sweat dripping down their six-pack abs and with shorts so short they could barely keep things in place. It was all I could do not to let my jaw hit the floor because (1) they looked like Greek gods and (2) I was insanely jealous that they were free to wear pretty much whatever they wanted without regard to anyone or anything.

There was a strict modesty dress code for all the girls. From funny sketches to sermons to small group discussions, *modest is hottest* was the catchphrase we ladies lived by. We were taught it was our duty to protect our brothers in Christ from falling into sexual temptation and sin.

In addition to being responsible for our own sexual purity, the sexual purity of the entire male population was evidently on our shoulders too. The weight of that responsibility felt crushing. But then again, we were constantly told that avoiding lust was harder for guys than for girls. If that was true, then it made our efforts noble. I was terrified of being the cause of any guy's falling into sin, so I did my best to cover up and preached to my campers, sisters, and any girl I met to follow suit.

I wish I could go back and apologize to every young girl I ever led to believe that it was her responsibility to uphold male sexual integrity. Maybe this is my opportunity to do just that.

In the moment it felt valiant, like we were taking a stand for the men in our lives. Only in hindsight do I see how disturbing of a narrative it was.

COVER YOURSELF

Camp wasn't the first or last time I heard about the importance of modesty. The messages I internalized from purity and church culture stacked up over the years. Something about the female body seemed inherently wrong, even dangerous. All at once women were too sexual and not sexual enough. For some reason it felt like women weren't allowed or considered to be sexual beings in the way that men were.[1] And since guys were *so weak* when it came to their desires, it became the responsibility of us women to keep them from sinning or doing something stupid. It was our cross to bear. Writer Chimamanda Ngozi Adichie has said it like this:

> We teach girls shame. "Close your legs." "Cover yourself." We make them feel as though by being born female they're already guilty of something. And so, girls grow up to be women who cannot see they have desire. They grow up to be women who silence themselves. They grow up to be women who cannot say what they truly think, and they grow up—and this is the worst thing we did to girls—they grow up to be women who have turned pretense into an art form.[2]

In hindsight, it's easy to see why for most of my life I felt like there was something distinctly offensive and inherently wrong about merely breathing. The narrative that the action or inaction of men is the responsibility of women, and that the crushing weight of their sexual integrity lies on our shoulders, is suffocating. *New York Times* journalist and author Peggy Orenstein argues, "At best, blaming girls' clothing for the thoughts and actions of boys is counterproductive. At worst, it's a short step from there to 'she was asking for it.'"[3] A message that revolves around the fear or threat of the female body and sexuality is one-dimensional and oppressive. It's a spiritual bypass that allows men to shirk responsibility.

It makes me wonder, do we have such a low view of men that we think them incapable of self-control? And do we think men are so beneath women that they are stunted and unable to take responsibility for their own sexual desire and integrity?

I happen to believe that when God created humanity, he created both men and women equally with dignity and honor.[4] Men are just as capable, strong, and competent as women. Let's stop blame-shifting and start empowering the men in our lives to be the men of vision and integrity we know God created them to be. Let's give them back what was theirs all along: the autonomy to take ownership over their sexuality. It's no wonder carrying the weight of male sexual purity has felt so crushing; it was never ours to carry.

If God did what He said He did in Genesis 1, making humanity in His image and likeness and calling it very good, that means the female body isn't bad, because God doesn't make bad things.[5] It also means that men and women are both sexual beings. The male body can be just as much of a turn-on as the female body. This is a both-and conversation, not either-or. When both sexes take responsibility for their sexuality, the core of the conversation around modesty shifts from shame and blame to empowerment and honor.

How, then, do we create a culture of honor between men and women without casting shame or judgment on either party?

THE MIDDLE GROUND

Before problem solving, we have to acknowledge the chasm of experiences between men and women. We live in a world of mixed messages, a world where women are hypersexualized from the time we're toddlers: "Only girls' fashions urge body consciousness at the very youngest ages. . . . Preschoolers worship Disney princesses, characters whose eyes are larger than their waists. No one is trying to convince eleven-year-old boys to wear itty-bitty booty shorts or bare their bellies in the middle of winter. . . . The pressure on young women to reduce their worth to their bodies and to see those bodies as a collection of parts that exist for others' pleasure" and "to continuously monitor their appearance"[6] is a reality for women that no man will ever fully understand.

We listen to songs that tell us to be "a lady in the street but a freak in the bed,"[7] and we live in a culture where men are allowed to and even encouraged to age. Wrinkles and gray hair are rugged and sexy. Women, on the other hand, are expected to be wrinkle free, cellulite free, gray hair free, and fit as a fiddle, with eternally perky breasts. We're supposed to be eternally young and *hott*. Ariel Levy, author of *Female Chauvinist Pigs*, says that "hotness" is the unique work of a woman.[8] A haunting example of this is the infamous "2015 *Vanity Fair* cover featuring Caitlyn Jenner, née Bruce. To announce her physical transition from male to female, the sixty-five-year-old appeared in a corset (from a store called Trashy Lingerie), breasts overflowing, lips glossed like an ingénue's. That image was often juxtaposed in the press with a picture of her as Bruce, hair lank with sweat, arms raised in triumph after winning Olympic Gold. As a man he used his body; as a woman, she displayed it."[9] The message underneath these modesty conversations implies that it's our responsibility as women to protect the male gaze, yet we're also told from the time we can barely talk that our bodies are objects to be displayed. All these expectations and mixed messages give me whiplash.

In her book *We Should All Be Feminists*, Chimamanda Ngozi Adichie laments over her first day teaching as a college professor. The anxiety wasn't over whether she was prepared to teach the material or adequately engage with her students, but over what she should wear. She knew stepping into a male-dominated space that she would have to prove her worth. She understood she would be judged more harshly than her male counterparts. If she was too girly or feminine, she wouldn't be taken seriously. She would have to work extra hard to gain their respect. Even though she loves being a woman—from wearing skirts with floral patterns and high heels to finding that perfect shade of lipstick to go with her look—she played it safe. Understanding that the professional standard in her field was the male wardrobe, she chose to wear what she called "an ugly suit."[10] Adichie notes, "A man going to a business meeting doesn't wonder about being taken seriously based on what he is wearing—but a woman does."[11]

The reality is that when a man wakes up in the morning and goes to his closet to get dressed, he never has to think, "What can I wear to make me less of a man, or how can I downplay my masculinity so as not to threaten or endanger women?" But as women, we constantly work to downplay our womanness, as if we forgo the red lipstick, maybe they won't notice we're female.

What's the answer, then? Is all modesty oppressive all the time? Do we wear whatever we want, whenever, however, and wherever we want to? I'm not convinced swinging to the other extreme will give us the freedom we long for. There has to be a middle ground between shaming women into hiding their bodies and advocating a free-for-all. What I've found is that truth often lies somewhere between the extremes. So much of our lives comes down to what's going on beneath the surface, which is why I believe the key to discerning that in-between ground comes through identifying heart, presence, and context.

HEART

Amid the 1990s college hookup scene, a young Jewish philosophy major, Wendy Shalit, had a wild revelation. In her groundbreaking book *A Return to Modesty*, she argues that keeping our clothes on and even saving sex for marriage (insert audible gasp) might be some of the most progressive and feminist decisions we could ever make.

Shalit offers two variations of modesty: "The first type of modesty is essentially developing an internal definition of self. When you know who you are, you don't generally feel a need to brag, to show your naked body to strangers, or to be involved physically with people who don't care about you. The second type of modesty entails recognizing the vulnerability of others and protecting it—as with a boy who receives a compromising photo of a girl and ignores orders to pass it on." Shalit further points out that genuine "modesty flows from the inside out, and in proportion to how much a person understands her own greatness and uniqueness."[12]

In other words, the physical reveals the climate of our internal landscape. Whereas the whole "modest is hottest" framework is rooted in shame and projects male sexual integrity onto women, Shalit argues that modesty starts and ends with love—the love of self and others. As Paul says to the Corinthians, love is dynamic and freeing because it "always protects, always trusts, always hopes, always perseveres."[13] When we're rooted in love, we cannot fail. It also means the burden of responsibility is on the individual, not the other.

Therefore, being grounded in who we are—our worth, value, and identity from the inside out—will transform how we, both men and women, approach our external lives. From this place, we are able to start asking questions like "How can I love myself well today?" and "How can I care for and be mindful of this person?" This self-worth can shape not only what we wear but also our thoughts, actions, words, and relationships to ourselves and others.

How is your internal self shaping the external experience of your life? Is your outer world in alignment with your inner hopes, dreams, purpose, and calling? If not, how can you become curious about that and then shift?

PRESENCE

I was recently speaking at an event and my bra strap kept falling down. Every time it slid down my arm and I reached to tuck it back onto my shoulder, it took me out of the moment. It was as annoying as it was distracting. If something is distracting to me, it's probably distracting to others too. I want people to hear my message as opposed to counting the number of times my bra strap slides down to my elbow. Whatever the clothing struggle is—tugging down a skirt that keeps riding up, wondering if my underwear is hanging out, or wondering whether a nipple is going to pop out of one of my tops—it's exhausting. I'd rather be fully present in the moment at hand than worried about a wardrobe malfunction. As Shalit says, modesty has the opportunity to give "me the freedom to think about things other than *Do I look OK?*"[14] The outfit I chose to wear onstage wasn't wrong or evil, but it was distracting for me and probably others too. Maybe our clothing choices aren't a case of right or wrong but of context. And context is everything.

CONTEXT

Would I wear a bathing suit at the beach? Yes. Would I wear it to a job interview? No. Would I wear a fun skirt and sassy top out for a night on the town? You bet. Would I wear that same outfit if I were preaching on a Sunday? No. Is this living a duplicitous lifestyle? No. It's using wisdom to discern the context of a given social situation.

On top of social context, we have to take note of the cultural context we're in. I currently live in a part of Brooklyn where there is a large population of Hasidic Jews. Year-round, these women don't wear anything that reveals their knees, elbows, midriffs, or collarbones. They also cover their real hair with a wig and often also a hat or scarf out of modesty. I'll never forget when I first moved to the neighborhood and my roommate went for a run in her leggings and sports bra top. She turned a corner and stumbled into what looked like a synagogue service just letting out. Parents literally shielded their children's eyes from her. Even though her workout pants went to her ankles and only two inches of her stomach were showing, she never felt more naked. She burst through the door of our tiny Brooklyn apartment, mortified.

One of my most fabulous and fashion-forward friends recently traveled to Morocco. She wore simple long dresses and scarves over her head, not out of obligation but out of respect and honor for the culture and people she was visiting.

Taking a posture of mindfulness and consideration of others is a kindness that helps foster a culture of honor wherever we go. When we acknowledge the spaces we're in and hold others in high regard, the modesty narrative shifts from being a tool to oppress the female body to an intentional expression of honor.

We're able to move forward and be practical when we're aware of both the context we're in and the heart behind our actions. For example, do I wear a bikini because I like it or because that's what's been marketed to me by society? Do I look for external validation (spoiler alert: we all do at times, don't we?), or do I wear something because I feel good and confident in it?

Are there situations and circumstances where less clothing can be freeing and empowering, say, when it's a thousand degrees outside and you work at a sports camp? And other circumstances where choosing to cover up can feel equally as freeing and empowering?

These questions aren't easy, and some of them may make you uncomfortable. But growth happens the moment we choose to leave our comfort zones. Choosing to dig deep into these questions and to step into the tension will equip you to navigate this conversation from a place of nuance and honesty.

Please hear me: nothing I do or do not wear ever gives anyone permission to make unwanted advances toward me. In addition to that, especially since we live in a global social media world, it's impossible to generalize modesty. When we make modesty about women wearing one-piece bathing suits and fingertip-length shorts—as if these are biblical mandates—we fall massively short. After all, I'm pretty sure a one-piece would have been scandalous in Jesus's day.

Modesty isn't about a set list of dos and don'ts; it's about a posture of the heart and the expression of love and kindness toward all people. All those years ago at camp, instead of the guys having a free-for-all, while the girls worked hard to stay covered up, I wish we had been able to sit down with both guys and girls and have a conversation about what honoring each other through our wardrobe would look like.

Modesty chooses to hold the self and others in high regard and is committed to cultivating a culture of honor. It's being rooted in our worth and identity; it's choosing to be kind and to love ourselves and others well. Even if it wasn't the intention, I think modesty was used as a teaching point to control and shame not only me but millions of women. Weaponizing modesty to shame people is highly problematic and falls incredibly short of God's heart for humanity. But just because modesty was hijacked by a chunk of the church doesn't mean we need to throw out the whole idea; it just means it needs to be redefined.

TAKE IT FURTHER

1. When you were growing up, what were some of the messages, explicit or implicit, that you learned about the female and male bodies?
2. What narratives were you taught about modesty? How have these beliefs shaped the way you view yourself, your body, sexuality, and desire? How have they shaped your view of men?
3. Reflect on whether certain aspects of modesty are still valuable to you and why.

Chapter Three

GUYS DON'T LIKE GIRLS LIKE ME

IS MY FEMININITY A LIABILITY?

As an evangelical girl, the one thing I could not be was me.

—Brenda Marie Davies

My great-grandma was a single mother and one of the first female journalists at her South Texas town paper.

Her daughter, my "gaw-gaw," bought a big yellow school bus when my dad was little. As kids hopped aboard the bus, they gave her a nickel for the ride. When moms were known for homemaking, she had a nanny and was out pounding the pavement.

My mom's mother, my grandma, lived all over the world as an Air Force wife. She raised her four children mainly solo while my grandpa was on assignment for months on end. She would put on lavish dinner parties, talent shows, and fashion shows on the Air Force bases. She was an incredible artist too. Fashion brands would hire her to draw sketches of their new collections for the Sunday paper. She was even flown out to New York City once by the brand Halston.

When my parents got divorced, my stay-at-home mom

enrolled in junior college, worked part-time in retail, picked up all four kids from school, and made a homemade meal that was ready every single night at six o'clock on the dot. After reading us stories and tucking us into bed, she'd stay up well into the night, reading books on finance. She taught herself how to build her own investment portfolio from scratch.

Strong women run in my family. Perseverance, strength, creativity, and that fierce go-getter spirit are in my DNA because of them.

When I became a Christian, it never occurred to me that I would need to downplay my strengths to fit within the social scripts of Western evangelical Christian culture. The need to downplay my strengths was subtle at times, and hard to pinpoint. In fact, it was so visible that it had become invisible. But once I saw it, I couldn't unsee it.

Two and a half years into college, I was still new to my faith, and all I wanted to do was learn as much as I could about Jesus. I constantly pored through the pages of my Bible and read theology books and commentaries. I'd go to my friends, mentors, and pastors with mile-long lists of questions about Christianity. I couldn't get enough. When I found there were Christian colleges with majors dedicated to studying the Bible, I knew I had to go. I left my full-ride tennis scholarship at a huge Division 1 school and transferred to a Baptist Bible college on the outskirts of Dallas that was smaller than my high school.

When I made the decision to become a Bible major, I received more than one metaphorical pat on the head from people at church, implying how cute it was that I wanted to study the Bible even though I'd never be able to preach since I was a woman. It felt condescending and also confusing because the Jesus I was learning about in the Bible seemed to be very pro women.

I'd sit in the front row of all my classes with one hand furiously taking notes and the other relentlessly in the air. I'd ask questions about how to reconcile the existence of a good God with the presence of evil in the world, while the guys were all but picking their noses in the back, arguing over which interpretation of the Bible was the best. I remember thinking that if these were our future pastors, we were in real trouble.

The longer I was a Christian, the more I noticed certain patterns.

Why were all the pastors at my church men? Why were mostly women in charge of the nursery and kids, but rarely high school–aged ministries and beyond? Why were the people in the decision-making rooms of the churches I attended mainly men (and white men, at that)? Why was it that many of the gifted women I knew kept quiet and let their husbands have the spotlight? Why were the leaders of worship bands almost always men, while women seemed designated to harmonies and backup vocals and the occasional solo? Why did I see women preaching from the stage only if it was a women's event?

It also seemed like my married girlfriends were somehow safer than singles. They were given more access to leadership roles as though a husband provides some sort of spiritual safety net that us single girls simply don't have. I also saw churches with husband-and-wife teams, but never once a church led by a group of singles, let alone a single woman.

Underneath the questions I have incessantly received over the years, like "How are you still single?" it feels like people are trying to figure out if something is wrong with me since I haven't been snatched up yet. Why aren't my single guy friends asked the same sort of questions? For some reason, there's little worry about the single Christian guys in my age range. Guys get a hall pass from all the questions about meeting "the one" because people can see that they're focused on building their lives and careers. Why are women pressured to get married and conditioned to aspire to marriage in a way that men aren't?

Why does so much of the Christian culture I experience feel like a boys-only club? Over the years, I realized that these questions didn't arise for me just at church or Bible school. From my barely-there dating life to my career, for some reason, as a woman, I constantly felt less than, outside of the club, and like I was given fewer opportunities than the men around me in the same life stage.

THE SURFER BOY

After college I worked in the nonprofit world for a few years. It was there I decided I wanted to pursue a career in photography. With zero experience, I somehow landed a job in Newport Beach, California, working as an assistant for one of the top photographers in the nation. Orange County was basically Dallas, Texas, at the beach. There were megachurches on every other corner and beautiful women dressed to the nines, and it was very conservative. I referred to it as the second Bible Belt.

One night at a beach bonfire, I met someone. He was the archetype of a Southern California guy: tall, athletic surfer with shaggy blond hair who rode through town on his longboard. When he asked me on a date a few weeks later, I was shocked. He was the first guy to ask me out in almost seven years. That alone made me feel giddy and excited.

On paper he fit the bill of everything I was looking for in a Christian guy. He had a grown-up job when most other SoCal guys were part-time actors trying to make it big in Hollywood. He would cook dinner for me and call me on days we didn't see each other, and he even mentored high school boys. Sometimes when we drove down the Pacific Coast Highway to go hiking in Laguna Beach, one hand on the steering wheel, the other interlaced with my fingers, he'd give me this look. Without a shadow of doubt, I knew he thought I was the one.

Everything in me wanted to like him. But when he kissed me, I felt nothing romantic for him. Even still, it felt so nice to be liked, and he did everything right. So I decided to give it some time to see if my feelings would develop. But I was up and down, hot and cold, and in constant inner turmoil about the whole thing. The poor guy. Looking back, I took him on quite the emotional roller coaster. After months of trying to make it work, I finally knew I wasn't going to get there with him.

As I drove to his house after work one night, there was a pit in my stomach. Oblivious, he hugged me, and we walked hand in hand to a park down the street. We sat on swings next to each other, and not knowing how to start the conversation, I just blurted it out. I told him I didn't know why, but I didn't have feelings for him. It was the whole "it's not you, it's me" scenario, except for the first time in my life, I was the one giving the speech. He sat on the swing and looked straight ahead. He was blindsided, and I hated that I was hurting him. He didn't have much to say, so he got up and walked me back to my car. As we said goodbye, he looked me in the eye and asked me if I thought I would ever find what I was looking for. I told him I sure hoped so. As I drove off, it felt like I exhaled for the first time in months. I felt relieved.

A few days later he ran into my best friend at a coffee shop and told her that Christian guys don't like girls like me—girls who are outspoken and have big dreams and career aspirations. He said Christian guys prefer girls who are teachers or work part-time at coffee shops. I had half a mind to go punch him in the face for degrading not only me but also teachers and baristas. What he was really saying was that Christian guys want women who put their lives on hold until they get a diamond ring on their finger and live to exist for the men in their lives.

What was I supposed to do? Sit around like a princess trapped in a castle until my knight in shining armor came and saved me? I had a calling on my life and bills to pay. Hiding out in my prayer closet until "the one" magically discovered me was not in the cards for me (nor did I want it to be).

A year later he was married to a cute Christian girl, and now they have a houseful of cute blond surfer kids. Here I am almost a decade later . . . single.

Was he right? Do Christian guys not like women like me?

SMALL, INVISIBLE, AND IN THE CORNER

The fancy photographer I worked for at the time shot New York Fashion Week twice a year. After I put in my time for a few years and begged him relentlessly, he finally let me go. I'll never forget photographing my first runway show in New York City.

We woke up at the crack of dawn to get to the venue in Chelsea to shoot the Monique Lhuillier show. You don't know claustrophobia until you've been crammed into a photographers' pit at New York Fashion Week. To have a spot, I had to sit between the legs of a hairy old man who kept trying to grope me. But it was either that or no spot.

As models walked down the runway in gowns worth more than my college education, often in shoes so small that their feet would bleed, the male photographers would hurl insults and heckle them. Most of these girls weren't more than sixteen years old. I was horrified. After the first show, which I totally bombed, a female photographer in her late fifties pulled me aside and coached me. She said my timing was off and to make sure I looked at the models' feet to see when I needed to take my next shot. We were the only two women in the pit. I didn't have much, but I knew I had an ally in her.

One night the magazine we were shooting for was throwing an industry party at the Plaza Hotel in Manhattan. We pulled up in a yellow taxicab, climbed the red-carpeted stairs to the lobby, and made our way through crowds of people into the party. A step and repeat was off to the left where paparazzi were photographing the VIP guests and celebrities, models walked around passing out glasses of Dom Pérignon and caviar, a jazz band played, and an open bar was available for the entire night. For a girl living on pennies as an assistant, this was the jackpot. I stuffed my purse with snacks for later. It was fancier than anything I had ever been to.

It was also the perfect opportunity to meet people in the industry and network with the other photographers. Throughout the night I went up to group after group of the male photographers I had been shooting with all day, but it was as though there was an impenetrable wall. Either I was ignored or they would immediately start talking about their wives as if I were trying to break apart their marriage. After hours of this treatment, I gave up. I sat in a corner and babysat my boss's camera gear while he chatted the night away with photographers, magazine editors, and designers. It was humiliating.

The rest of the week was a blur. It was nonstop shooting on the hour, every hour, for twelve-plus hours a day for clients who wanted images, like, yesterday. Between shows I would edit images in the cab as we raced to snag a spot in the pit before the next show. Our nights were filled with parties and lavish client dinners where the bill was more than I made in an entire month. Then I'd head back to the hotel room in the wee hours of the morning to finish editing, sleep an hour or two, and repeat the whole thing the next day.

I left that first fashion week feeling defeated and alone. I didn't want to go back. Fighting for my place in a male-dominated industry was exhausting. I've never felt so small or invisible in my life.

From the church to the culture, my femininity felt like

a liability. I felt not enough and too much all at the same time. It was this perfect gridlock that kept me playing small in my faith, relationships, and career. But everything changed when I discovered God's heart for women. Let me take you on a little journey through Scripture.

TAKE IT FURTHER

1. Which women in your family inspire you, and what have they taught you?
2. What are some of the messages you've internalized from the church and culture about being a woman?
3. Have you ever felt like your femininity is a liability? How so?

Chapter Four

THE TIME I BECAME A FEMINIST

GOD LOVES STRONG WOMEN

She has the audacity to act like the queen she is
and she doesn't complain about the myriad requests for her time
or going unrecognized
or the weight of the crown
because she knows it is the lightest load she will ever carry . . .

—*Danielle Bennett Simmons*

God created humanity to reflect what He's like to the world and in doing so expresses that both man and woman are very good.[1] Within the first pages of Scripture, God sets the precedent: men and women are equal in worth, value, and calling. There is no less than or better than. From the very beginning, women are woven throughout the God-story.

BRAVE WOMEN RUN IN OUR DNA

A little while after Eve, we meet Esther. She was an orphan turned queen and used her authority and influence to put a stop to the planned genocide of the Hebrew people.*

Then we have Ruth, the widow with nothing to her name who followed her mother-in-law, Naomi, to a foreign country. She worked the fields to survive and to provide food for Naomi and herself. Eventually she showed up at the house of her boss, Boaz, in the middle of the night and basically proposed to him.[2] Talk about bold. This would've been both scandalous and a completely provocative gesture. Let's be honest, it's pretty bold by today's standards too. When was the last time you heard of a woman going out in the middle of the night and sneaking into the house of a guy she wasn't even dating and asking him if he wanted to marry her?

Now, Boaz was a godly man and had an incredible reputation. Who knows why he didn't pursue Ruth? Maybe he thought he was too old for her or didn't want to take advantage of the position of power he had in her life, or perhaps he was insecure, fearing she'd reject him. Whatever the reason, to get together, Ruth had to make the first move. Their marriage was redemptive for both of them, and Ruth gave birth to a son, Obed. Naomi's community of women spoke life and destiny over her grandson: "He shall be to you a restorer of life and a nourisher."[3] Obed became the father of Jesse, who became the father of David, the guy who wrote most of the Psalms and was known as being a man after God's own heart.[4]

The line of David ultimately led to the birth of Jesus. God could have made anyone part of this lineage, but He used a courageous widow who wasn't afraid to scandalously go against the cultural and religious norms of her time to fulfill her calling. In Christian culture we frown upon any sort of romantic initiation from women, but Ruth's boldness didn't

---

* Just go ahead and read the entire book of Esther. You won't regret it.

bother God. On the contrary, God radically honored it. Her boldness became her legacy, which would reverberate through generations to come.

And then there's Hannah. She's one of my favorites. Her grand debut in Scripture is a declaration of her barrenness. She lived in a small farm town, and if you know anything about small towns, it's safe to assume everyone in her family and community would've known her secret. As a woman, her lot in life was to keep house and provide a male heir for her husband. She could have been thrown out on the streets or turned into a household slave for being unable to fulfill her wifely duties. No one would've blinked an eye. Imagine your infertility, perhaps the most tender and painful part of your story and something totally out of your control, being public knowledge and the thing that could land you on the streets!

Hannah was shamed and provoked relentlessly for her inability to conceive.[5] Her heart was shattered, and there were times she even refused to eat. Depression was her constant companion. Yet somehow, in a cultural moment when she had no voice or rights, she found favor. Her husband loved and adored her. He fought for her and tried to mend her broken heart.[6]

Year after year Hannah found herself in the house of the Lord, begging God for a child. She wept bitterly, made bargains with God, was anxiety ridden, and made such a scene that the priest Eli called her out for being drunk. When was the last time you prayed so desperately for God to break through in your life that someone would've mistaken you for being drunk?

When Eli rebuked her, Hannah's appropriate response, even if she had been wrongly accused, would have been to hang her head and bow out quietly. But Hannah stood up for herself and her cause. Her boldness moved the priest's heart to compassion, and he blessed her. Scripture says that sometime later

God remembered Hannah, and in due time she conceived and bore a son. She named him Samuel, which in Hebrew means "heard by God."

The story doesn't end there. Hannah ends up with not one but six children.[7] Her honesty and imperfect yet faithful persistence inspire me.

Then there's the famous Proverbs 31 poem honoring the godly woman. For a long time this model of the godly woman felt stifling to me, but that was before I did a deep dive of the text. The Proverbs 31 woman is a powerhouse. She is strong, thoughtful, trustworthy, and loves God. But the description of her doesn't stop there. She is a provider for her family. She gets up before the sun to get to work to feed her family and her staff.[8] The text says, "She considers a field and buys it; out of her earnings she plants a vineyard."[9] She also has her own fashion line that she sells in the city and to the merchants. So she's in investment property, owns a vineyard, and is a designer. These aren't cute side hobbies; they're profitable business ventures.[10] The Proverbs 31 woman is entrepreneurial and business savvy and shares the financial load with her husband. She is filled with wisdom, and when her children grow up, they, along with her husband, publicly praise her.[11] She is a respected leader in the community and has a powerful voice. When she speaks, people listen.[12]

God breathed authority and possibility over women in a time when they had little say culturally, economically, politically, and religiously. I can't believe how progressive this text is. The God of the Old Testament didn't silence or shame women. The women of the Old Testament are brave, courageous, sharp as tacks, fearless, risk-taking, and extremely influential. What a far cry from the mousy, quiet, submissive archetype of a godly woman I grew up hearing about in church.

All this, and we haven't even met Jesus yet. As we transition from the Old to the New Testament, this theme of God empowering and using women further solidifies, and Jesus leads the way.

HUMAN TO HUMAN

First, we can't skip over the fact that God could've used anyone in any way to reveal the Savior of the universe. However, God chose to use Mary, an engaged teenage woman with no money or status. And she was a virgin.[13]

During Jesus's ministry, He met midday with the woman at the well whose life was out of control. With five broken marriages and currently living with a man who wasn't her spouse, she was a social outcast. Not only that, she was a Samaritan woman, which meant by Jewish standards she was unclean. Jesus should've avoided her like the plague. Instead, we find Him spending time alone with her, looking her in the eyes, speaking directly to her, and offering her compassion and kindness. After their interaction, she left and told anyone who would listen about her encounter. Many people came to faith in Jesus through this woman's story.

Jesus wasn't afraid to be physically close to a woman, and He didn't care about what other people would think or the rumors that might circulate. He was more interested in connecting human to human with her than maintaining His reputation with the religious folk.[14]

Later we find that while it was culturally acceptable and in line with religious norms to condemn and even kill women caught in adultery, Jesus extended acceptance and friendship. He knelt next to the woman paraded through town for being caught in an affair. Instead of judgment, He met her with dignity and kindness. He wasn't ashamed to be associated with a woman caught in sexual scandal. What He cared about was her heart and restoring the humanity that had been stripped away by oppression and legalism.[15]

DO YOU SEE THIS WOMAN?

Then there's the sinful woman who cried at the feet of Jesus in the middle of a dinner party with a bunch of religious leaders.[16] Uninvited, she showed up anyway. With a flask of expensive perfume, she washed Jesus's feet with her tears, kissing them while wiping them dry with her hair. Out of modesty, women kept their hair up and covered unless they were alone with their husbands. Having her hair down and using it to wash the feet of Jesus was a highly sensual and deeply intimate exchange. There's no doubt the interaction would've been interpreted as having sexual undertones. To say the least, it would've been a provocative and awkward experience for everyone present.

Jesus interrupts it all by asking the religious leaders, "Do you see this woman?"[17] She was invisible to them, identified only by her shortcomings. To them she was a sinner, unworthy of being in their presence. Yet Jesus was unthreatened by her initiative, her physical touch, and her public display of affection. He calls them all out by saying, "I entered your house; you gave me no water for my feet, but she has wet my feet with her tears and wiped them with her hair. You gave me no kiss, but from the time I came in she has not ceased to kiss my feet. You did not anoint my head with oil, but she has anointed my feet with ointment. Therefore I tell you, her sins, which are many, are forgiven—for she loved much."[18]

Author Carrie Miles writes, "To Jesus women were more than sources of impurity, temptresses, wombs, servants, hostesses or whores."[19] Jesus didn't view the woman or her body as a problem to be solved or avoided. Instead, He highlighted the richness of her faith and held her up as an example to the religious who watched the whole scene soaked in their own pride and arrogance.

On the heels of this encounter, in Luke 8, we discover

women like Joanna and Susanna, who traveled with Jesus and helped fund his ministry.[20] Later, in the book of Acts, we meet influential women like Lydia, a successful business owner in a metropolitan city who helped fund and lead the early church.[21] There's also Phoebe, an early church leader Paul mentions in Romans.[22] The list goes on and on.

Finally, we can't dismiss the resurrection. Jesus could have revealed Himself to anyone in any way. But He chose to show Himself first to His close friend and confidant: Mary Magdalene. He met with her alone in a garden, a place where lovers would rendezvous. Even though, as theologian Dan Brennan writes, "he was a first-century Jew firmly situated in the social context of Palestine, Jesus' friendships with women were revolutionary."[23] And despite the pressure I'm sure He received from many sides, Jesus "didn't support narrow conformity to social boundaries out of consideration for public sensibilities."[24] I'm not insinuating that Jesus and Mary Magdalene were romantically involved; rather, it's interesting to pause and think about the depth of relationship Jesus had with women, both single and married. He chose to interact with women as whole beings instead of avoiding them as though they were threats.

Throughout the biblical narrative, strong women are an integral part of the story.

Women weren't dangerous to Jesus. Nor were they less than or second-class citizens to men. He didn't tell them to hide their bodies, quiet their voices, or stay at home, but rather invited them into His inner circles. Instead of being banished to the background, women were empowered with influence and authority. Risk-taking, out-of-the-box women who didn't have a place in cultural or religious circles had powerful roles to play in God's kingdom, and they flourished. They put their lives on the line for the gospel. The more I read the Bible, and the more I get to know this Jesus, the more liberated I feel as a woman.

We just can't escape it: God is for women.

Far too often and for far too long, the world—from culture all the way to the church—has spoken confining narratives over the lives of women. And those narratives have kept us small. We've been given fewer opportunities than men to use our God-given gifts, talents, and abilities while simultaneously told to stay quiet, to be content in the background, and that our life will be complete only if we have a spouse.

It's no wonder I was confused when I got to Bible college and so many people condescendingly patted me on the head. I didn't grow up in Christian culture, so I didn't know the norms yet. I didn't know the verses that had been taken out of context and used to keep women out of leadership roles.[25] The only thing I had was my Bible and story after story of God using brave, strong, and capable women to further His kingdom. When we put women in the corner and keep them out of decision-making rooms, leadership roles in the church, and CEO positions in business, we all suffer.

Remember how small I felt after photographing my first fashion week? As discouraged as I was, I kept going back.

WHAT'S IN A NAME?

A few years after shooting my first fashion week, I was hired to photograph my first big editorial campaign. The clients didn't know I had never been head shooter on anything close to an editorial. On my flight to New York City, I had to research how to use the equipment I rented for the shoot. I had never used studio lighting before and was terrified that with one wrong move I'd start a fire and burn the whole studio to the ground. I was in over my head, but at the same time something inside me lit up.

This was my chance.

For the first time, I hired the team, from the stylist to assistants to hair and makeup. I had been on enough sets where there was body shaming, gossip, and drama. I was committed to not letting that happen on my watch. Out of my own pocket, I ordered breakfast, lunch, and snacks to make sure no one was hungry.

The client rented an industrial loft space with exposed brick and old wooden floors that had been used for photo shoots in magazines like *Vogue*. The girl modeling for us had been on the cover of magazines and walked runways all over the world. There must have been hundreds of thousands of dollars' worth of gowns and jewelry brought in for the day; it all felt surreal.

I was a ball of nerves, but as we started shooting, the day flew by. Between shots I would chat with our model and found out she had a two-month-old son. Just weeks after his birth, she walked the runways at New York Fashion Week. How this woman had a newborn and was fitting into designer dresses was beyond me.

As the shoot wrapped and everyone started packing up, our model came up to me in her black combat boots and leather jacket that made her look both casual and like the chicest person I had ever seen. In a quiet voice she said, "Thank you so much for asking me my name today. No photographer has ever done that before." Before I could say much, she hugged me and then ran outside to catch her cab home. Choking back tears, I stood there stunned.

The editorial was picked up on two national campaigns and for the cover of a magazine. The shoot was pivotal for my career, but it also showed me something else. If the men who photographed that model were anything like the majority of men in that first fashion week pit, then no wonder she felt safe and seen by me. In an industry dominated by men, I had something different to offer: my feminine heart and perspective.

FOR SUCH A TIME AS THIS

Now, finally, back to my surfer boy. There may be men out there who are threatened by purpose-filled women. And you know what? What a shame. They're missing out. But hear me: there *are* good men out there who love women like you and me. I know this because I have a lot of friends married to men like this. More importantly, you need to know this: God isn't threatened by you. As women, and men for that matter, the best thing we can do is embrace who we are and fully be the humans God designed us to be. You may be misunderstood, and that's okay. Live a courageous life, and never apologize for that.

The good news is this: The God story is a redemptive story. It's one where He invites all hands to be on deck. If we want to restore what's been broken or misunderstood, it's going to take both men and women walking forward hand in hand with humility and strength. So, no, I won't say what some might think I'm going to say, that the "future is female." The future is all people living in alignment with their giftings and callings. Only when we're running the race of life together in unity are we fully able to collaborate with God in moving the needle of restoration forward.

If you have ever felt dismissed by the church, or like a threat to the sexual integrity of men for merely existing, or as though your voice or leadership has no place in the church simply because you are a woman, or a single woman at that, I am so sorry this has been your experience. Those attitudes are small minded and not God's heart for you. Just as Jesus challenged the Pharisees to *see* the woman in front of them as an integrated, whole person, it's time we did the same.

I want you to know I see you.

I hear you.

Like the brave women before you, you have been placed in

"such a time as this" to accomplish that which only God can accomplish through you.[26]

You are worthy.

You are enough.

Your womanness is priceless.

Your femininity is magic.

And we need you—your voice, your perspective, and your leadership.

If we hold Scripture in high esteem, then in regard to women, among many other things, it's baffling how out of alignment much of the Western church is with the heart of God. As a whole, we have to do better.

All along, this truth has been hidden between the lines from Esther to Ruth to Hannah, Joanna, Lydia, and the countless fiery and passionate women throughout Scripture, and it has forever changed me: my femininity isn't a liability; it's my greatest asset. It turns out, the thing about me that has felt like my biggest hindrance in faith, dating, life, my career, and everything in between is my secret sauce.

As a Christian woman, I used to think *feminism* was a dirty word. But then I did my homework. At the core, a feminist is a person who believes in the social, political, legal, and economic equality of the sexes.[27] (I would add religious equality to that as well.) In that case, I'm pretty sure I'm a feminist. And I think Jesus might be one too.

TAKE IT FURTHER

1. Which woman from Scripture do you resonate with most, and why?
2. Can you describe a specific situation in your life in which your femininity was an asset?
3. Up until this point, what have been your thoughts on feminism? Have they shifted at all? How so?

Chapter Five

SUBMIT TO MY HUSBAND . . . WHAT DOES THAT EVEN MEAN?

SUBMISSION, PERSONAL AGENCY, AND GENDER ROLES

I didn't fall in love with you. I walked
into love with you, with my eyes wide open,
choosing to take every step along the way.
—*Kiersten White*

Recently, I met a girlfriend for drinks in the city. She arrived late and was flustered. It wasn't the frantic energy of New York living that was dragging her down this particular day, but a conversation she just had with her mentor. Her mentor told her that as a Christian wife, she needed to submit to her husband's needs as Ephesians 5 teaches. More explicitly the woman said it was my friend's *biblical duty* to make sure she kept his belly full in the kitchen and kept him sexually satisfied in the bedroom.

My friend, who loves God and loves her husband and by her account has a great sex life, felt both infuriated and confused.

And rightfully so. If this is what it means to be a godly wife, then count me out.

Underneath the language clothed in Christian jargon, I hear a spiritually manipulative message that says: a woman doesn't own her sexuality; it exists for and belongs to her husband. Is this what Ephesians 5 means when Paul tells wives to submit to their husbands? I hope not. Where is the personal agency for the woman in regard to her body and sexuality?

Let's take a look at the text:

> Wives, submit yourselves to your own husbands as you do to the Lord. For the husband is the head of the wife as Christ is the head of the church, his body, of which he is the Savior. Now as the church submits to Christ, so also wives should submit to their husbands in everything.
>
> Husbands, love your wives, just as Christ loved the church and gave himself up for her to make her holy, cleansing her by the washing with water through the word, and to present her to himself as a radiant church, without stain or wrinkle or any other blemish, but holy and blameless. In this same way, husbands ought to love their wives as their own bodies. He who loves his wife loves himself. After all, no one ever hated their own body, but they feed and care for their body, just as Christ does the church—for we are members of his body. "For this reason a man will leave his father and mother and be united to his wife, and the two will become one flesh." This is a profound mystery—but I am talking about Christ and the church. However, each one of you also must love his wife as he loves himself, and the wife must respect her husband.
>
> —*Ephesians 5:22–33*

Before I attempt to unpack a wildly misunderstood passage, let me say that this is a tough text. I thought writing this chapter would take me a week, and here I am almost two months later, because I've had to wrestle with the text. I've read it again and again until I've gone cross-eyed, and then gone back to it again. I've talked with pastors and prayed for wisdom and insight to make sure I don't bend the text to make it say what I want it to say, because if I'm being honest, as a single woman living in New York City in 2020, at first glance, this text makes me cringe. Submit to my husband? Barf. It feels archaic.

And if one of the overarching themes of the biblical narrative is that God is for women, there has to be more to this text than first meets the eye.

BIBLE STUDY 101

We have to talk hermeneutics 101: the who, what, when, where, and why of Bible study and interpretation. Before we can apply any text to our lives today, we need to know that it was written to a specific people, at a specific time, and for a specific purpose. So first things first, who wrote the Ephesians 5 passage, who did they write it for, and why?

Ephesians 1:1 tells us the apostle Paul wrote this letter to a group of Christians at the church in Ephesus. Through cross-referencing other passages and historical study, we know Paul wrote to the church of Ephesus while he was under house arrest in approximately AD 62. This was about thirty years after Jesus died, which means the church was still young.* When I was new

* When the who, what, where information is not readily available in the text, not to worry. Many study Bibles have commentary with this information, and if you don't have one of those Bibles, there are a ton of Bible commentaries and studies online. Thank You, Jesus, for Amazon Prime. Logos Bible Software and the YouVersion app are great resources. Teachers like Beth Moore and Priscilla Shirer also have incredibly extensive Bible studies on certain books of the Bible. Truth be told, I learned more Bible history in Beth Moore's Bible study on Daniel than I did in my Old Testament class on Jeremiah in Bible college.

to my faith, I needed a lot of encouragement, mentorship, good theology, and practical advice. Paul offered all of the above in this letter.

Another thing to take into consideration when we approach the Bible is the cultural context in which a given text was written. As the Roman capital of Asia in the first century and with a harbor booming with trade, Ephesus was a metropolitan city and a hub for modern culture. Because of that, it was filled with a wide range of economic opportunities. This meant it was filled with socioeconomic, religious, and ethnic diversity. Culturally, women had little to no rights. They weren't allowed to vote, and the majority had only a basic level of education. Many women weren't even taught how to read. They had little to no independence or autonomy and often went from living under their father's roof to living under the authority of their husband.

The expectation was that women would stay at home, provide a male heir, and take care of the children. Marriage looked more like a business deal and was often loveless. Men were not expected to be faithful. It was commonplace for husbands to have multiple lovers and mistresses, while the wives were expected to look the other way. Women were a commodity. They belonged to men and were not seen as equals.

Ephesus was also home to the temple dedicated to the worship of the Roman goddess Diana (or known in Greek as Artemis), where ritual prostitution was performed as an act of worship. The temple prostitutes were primarily enslaved women, their bodies acting as the object of a transaction for someone else's spiritual elevation and enlightenment.

It was into this cultural climate and context that Paul wrote Ephesians. The entire letter is jam-packed with encouragement, theology, and practical wisdom that made it accessible and implementable to a young community of Christians living in a fast-paced metropolis. Throughout his letter, Paul constantly points back to Jesus as the source of wisdom, purpose, and salvation.[1] He addresses everything from the church to the city to parenting to work to marriage, with a repeated theme of unity throughout. With verses such as, "Remember that you were at that time separate from Christ . . . without hope and without God,"[2] Paul levels the playing field of humanity by dismantling any sense of hierarchy among people.

Paul's message is clear: In the kingdom of God, every human matters. No one is better than anyone else. Every human needs Jesus, and because of that, we are all equal. For the people of Ephesus, this was a bold and subversive message!

Paul encourages the church to walk in love and submit to each other not out of obligation but out of their love for Jesus.[3] He speaks unity into every area of their lives, from work to friendship to family to marriage. Pulled outside its context, the instruction for wives to submit to their husbands looks like another attempt to degrade and control women under the guise of spirituality. But when we take a closer look, this passage was a wildly progressive call to both women and men, not only in the first century but also today.

Yes, the text does invite women to submit to their husbands. However, we can't just pull any phrase or verse out of the Bible void of its context and place the meaning we want onto it. That's not wisdom; it's spiritual manipulation. We have to look at the whole of the text.

In a time of loveless marriages and when women were dominated, viewed as less than, and had few rights, Paul challenges Christian men to be countercultural. He beckons men to love their wives, to honor and be faithful to them because, unlike the current culture they lived in, in the kingdom of God, women have infinite worth and esteem. This message was radical and even offensive to those living with the first-century societal norms surrounding women and marriage. But Paul doesn't stop at telling husbands to merely love their wives. He takes it a step further and tells them to love their wives as Jesus loved the church.

This message would've been explicitly clear to the early church: Jesus laid down His life for the church.

A LOVE LIKE THIS

Jesus's life was one of submission. He expressed His love for the church by submitting to the call of God the Father on His life to offer His life in service of humanity. During His life, Jesus fought for, protected, and served the church. When the religious elite tried to take advantage of people, Jesus flipped tables and took a public stand against the abuse of power taking place in the church.[4] Jesus was friends with those ostracized by society and hung out with folks that the religious elite wouldn't be caught dead with. And even though He was God, He got on his knees and washed caked dirt off the feet of those He ate with, as if He were a hired servant.[5] Jesus didn't have a god complex or abuse His power to get ahead, but used His leadership and influence to humbly serve and love others. He fought for the oppressed and brought justice, healing, and restoration to seemingly impossible circumstances.

Jesus was also a man of His word. If He said someone was healed, they were healed.[6] He remained loyal even when it was inconvenient, even when it would cost Him His life. When Jesus was arrested and His closest friends and allies turned their backs on Him and denied association with Him, He still chose love. When He knew His path was to die and leave the earth, He made sure we, the church, would be cared for by giving us the gift of the Holy Spirit.[7] Jesus backed up His words with actions. He wasn't only willing to die for the church, He actually did. Jesus took the bullet for humanity.

Then, because He loved humanity so much, He came back

to life and visited His community for forty days before going to heaven. His final battle cry before leaving earth was a reminder that He was and is Immanuel, God with us. He has resolved never to leave us.[8]

Jesus's love is steady, stable, secure, and unconditional. He has vision and character and is trustworthy, tender yet strong, and humble but not a pushover. He never has ulterior, selfish, or impure motives. Jesus pursues our hearts but never manipulates, dominates, or forces His way into our lives. In essence, Jesus is the perfect gentleman.

And this is the example of how a husband is to love his wife.

Something happens when we collide with a love like this; it changes us. Paul says this kind of unconditional love is sanctifying; it makes us whole.[9] True love is restorative and transformative; it exposes unhealthy patterns and takes us on a path toward healing.

The Ephesians 5 text isn't about a husband dominating, fixing, or saving his wife, nor is it about wives blindly submitting to their husbands or keeping their bellies and sexual appetites satisfied; it's about an outward-focused, radical sort of mutual love that is like healing waters washing over the trauma and wounds of our past, leading us into more and more health and wholeness.

It's also not about perfection. Jesus is God and we are not. There isn't a guy out there who's going to be able to live up to Jesus. Let's be grace filled and have space for the people in our lives to be on a journey. The goal isn't perfection but a heart committed to loving well.

EQUAL PRIORITIES

While the call for husbands to love their wives as Jesus loved the church is a high one, Paul still isn't done with the men. He then reminds husbands to love their wives as they love their own bodies. The emphasis is that unlike the marriages of the times, in the Christian marriage, the wants and needs of the wife are of equal priority to the husband's. Amid a myriad of things, this means that if a man wants to experience pleasure in the bedroom, then it must be an equal priority to him that the woman does too. I'd even go further and say that, in light of Jesus's servant posture with which he loved the church, the husband would put his wife's pleasure before his own.

As we dive into the Ephesians 5 passage, it's important that its messages are in alignment with the overarching narrative of Scripture, because Scripture will never contradict itself. We can again go back to Genesis 1 and see that both genders are made fully in the image of God, which means that both have identical rights, value, and worth. One doesn't have privilege over the other.

If the creator of the universe advocates for equality between the sexes, it's time we caught up.

MY SEXUALITY BELONGS TO ME

First Samuel 16:7 says humans look at the external, but God "looks at the heart." In the New Testament, Jesus says that even though some of us may do all the right things, we can be strangers to God.[10] From the Old Testament to the New, the biblical precedence is that God doesn't want people to serve Him out of duty. He wants our hearts, not just behavior modification, and He honors and advocates for personal agency. This means I can choose from a place of freedom and autonomy, not fear or obligation, to freely give my body, mind, and spirit to God or to my husband or anyone else, for that matter. Paul, in Romans 12:1, affirms this when he invites people "in view of God's mercy, to offer your bodies as living sacrifices, holy and pleasing to God—this is your spiritual act of worship" (NIV 1984). Paul understands it's not his right to demand that we do anything with our bodies but that it's a personal choice to give yourself to anyone or anything—even to God. This goes all the way back to the garden with Adam and Eve. God created the opportunity for Adam and Eve to choose God or the Tree of Knowledge of Good and Evil. From the very beginning God never forced his hand but honored and allowed space for humans to choose. When we lose the power of choice, we lose part of our humanness. After all, we're humans, not robots. And is love really love without choice? Therefore, my spirit and mind and also my body and sexuality belong to me. I may choose to share my body and sexuality with another person or not. And even when and if I do, at no point does that mean it belongs to or exists for them.

In a culture that practiced sex in temples with enslaved women, the idea that a woman's body and sexuality belonged first and foremost to her was just another factor that differentiated the Christian faith and made the ways of Jesus unbelievably radical and progressive.

Ephesians 5 ends with a big secret revealed: human marriage is supposed to be a reflection of Jesus's relationship with the church. People should see a Christian marriage and be in awe of the love of God. It's clear: the God of the Bible honors and respects our value, worth, bodies, sexuality, and personal agency. If this is how relationship unfolds between God and people, then marriage should follow suit.

At first when I read this passage, I cringed, but now I look at it and am dumbfounded by how truly compelling marriage can be. Can you imagine how powerful and transformative it would be to love and be loved like that? I would have such a high level of trust and respect for a man so humbled and submitted to God's call on his life, committed to sacrificing his life and his preferences, and devoted to a life of loving and serving me and our family. Just the thought of it overwhelms me.

When I take into account the culture and context of the text, Ephesians 5 seems less about gender roles and more about casting a countercultural, robust vision of a radical marriage that is bursting at the seams with mutual love, support, honor, and submission.

My aunt and uncle have been married for almost forty years. They still flirt with each other, and you can tell they genuinely like to be around each other. Coming from a broken home, I've looked at their marriage and studied it over the years, as if they're some strain of human that can breathe underwater. One day I asked my aunt how they've lasted for so long. She said that my uncle really doesn't like waking up early for work. Even so, he has done it faithfully for decades. Every night before my aunt goes to bed, she puts coffee grounds and water in the coffeepot and sets an automatic timer so the coffee will start brewing right before my uncle's alarm goes off. When he stumbles groggily into the kitchen, there's a fresh pot of coffee ready for him. It's a small, almost insignificant gesture. In the grand scheme of things, it saves him less than five minutes, but what matters is the heart behind it. She doesn't have to do it, nor does he expect her to. But because she loves him, it's her joy to do so. She then told me they both wake up every day with the goal to outserve the other person, from the small to big things in life. It's matter of fact to them that love and service go hand in hand.

BYE, ARCHIE BUNKER

Let me be crystal clear: the Ephesians 5 text isn't a one-sided call for wives to submit like a 1950s housewife to their misogynistic Archie Bunker of a husband. Nor is wives' submission a theme we see throughout Scripture. When we look at Ephesians 5 in context and in its entirety, along with the greater scope of the Bible narrative, we see a relational precedence of an outward-focused sort of love built upon layers of trust, equality, integrity, honor, and respect. There is an undeniable call for a mutual submission between spouses. I would even dare say that the call on the husband carries greater weight and implication than that on the wife. I'm invited to respect him, but he's supposed to die for me!

Too many women have been spiritually manipulated into denying their own desires and needs and staying in abusive and toxic relationships because of poor theology. This narrative is not only unbiblical, it promotes one-sided sexual encounters and relationships, silences conversations around consent, and ultimately encourages rape culture.

After taking all this into account, let's go back to my friend whose mentor reminded her of her "wifely duties." Her mentor's instruction sounded more reminiscent of first-century Roman culture than any sort of biblical teaching on marriage.

If we're going to teach Ephesians 5, let's go ahead and teach the whole thing.

Alright, I've spent the last few chapters identifying and deconstructing some of the toxic and damaging narratives I grew up learning about in Christian culture. Like I said from the get-go, we have to look back before we can look forward.

Now that we've done that, let's spend some time reimagining what a renewed, healthy sexual ethic could look like.

TAKE IT FURTHER

1. Up until this point, what have you been taught about gender roles within marriage?
2. Did anything surprise you or resonate with you about the Ephesians 5 teaching? Was there anything new that you hadn't thought of before?
3. What does it feel like to know that your sexuality belongs to you and that God honors your personal agency?

PHASE TWO

The Reconstruction

Chapter Six

STAY OUT TILL YOU MAKE OUT

THE MYTH THAT YOU ARE YOUR DESIRE

Perhaps when we find ourselves
wanting everything it is because we are
dangerously near to wanting nothing.
—*Sylvia Plath*

My Christian friends and I called it "stay out till you make out." It felt edgy but still safe. My kind of rebellion. One winter night in my twenties, I went dancing with a group of girls at a bar in Brooklyn. Almost immediately a cute blond and I locked eyes from across the room. We found our way to each other, danced a few songs, and started kissing. I found my "stay out till you make out" guy, and it wasn't even midnight. I didn't know his name, and it didn't matter to me.

Then out of nowhere, a thought burst into my head: "I could be kissing my hand right now, and it would feel the same." In case you're wondering, that's an annoying thought to have mid-makeout. I tried to stop it, but it was too late. The runaway train of my brain had left the station.

Why am I kissing this guy?

And why do I feel nothing toward him?

Aren't I entitled to have a little fun?

It's not like I'm sleeping around or anything.

But is this really what I want?

Talk about a mood killer.

THE POWER OF CHOICE

Like the siren's luring call, culture beckons us to surrender to our desires, to allow them to lead the way. It's as if once the wheels of desire have been set into motion, there's no stopping it. The message we receive is subtle but clear: I am my desire. We're taught to live "our truth" and do what feels good to us.

If it itches, scratch it.

If you have a hunger, feed it.

Underneath it all, desire is in the driver's seat. But if we're really living our best lives, why are we a lonelier, more medicated, anxious, depressed, burned out, and addicted culture than ever before?

In his book *Sex God,* author Rob Bell talks about a common Greek phrase that Paul references in 1 Corinthians 6:13: "food for the stomach and the stomach for food." The Greeks, Bell says, "understood a person to be a collection of physical needs. . . . They concluded that sex is just like food, so when a man was 'hungry,' he would go to a prostitute, saying, 'food for the stomach . . .'" This ideology doesn't sound too different from our current "do what feels good . . . live your truth" culture. The Achilles' heel of this belief system, however, "is that it's rooted in a low view of human nature. The assumption behind it is that people are going to have sex because they can't help themselves. This perspective is presented as freedom and honesty and just being who you are and doing what comes naturally, but it's built on the belief that certain things are inevitable. What it really teaches is that people cannot transcend the physical dimensions of their existence. It views people much like animals."[1] This may be why when it comes to sex and physical intimacy, we say things like, "I don't know . . . it just happened," or "We couldn't help ourselves."

But is that true? Can we really not help ourselves? Or as Bell puts it, "Are we just the sum of our urges?"[2]

If being human means we don't have restraint over our desires, then let's face it, we'd have a real-life *Hunger Games* meets *Lord of the Flies* situation on our hands.

But God created humans distinct from animals. There may be overwhelming similarities at times, but the truth remains: humans aren't animals, which means we are more than the sum of our desires. Humans have logic, decision-making skills, will-power, and resolve. We have the capacity to practice restraint, and we can say no even to good and beautiful things when we have a vision for something greater in the future. One of the most fundamental things about being human is the power of choice.

For over a decade I've been a wedding photographer, and I've been a bridesmaid seventeen times. In no exaggeration, I've either photographed or attended literally hundreds of weddings. Yet with every wedding I experience, I still am struck by how profound it is that even in this instant-gratification, do-what-feels-good culture, millions of people every year decide to get married.

Just getting to the aisle is a complete miracle. So much has to line up for two people to first meet, then come together, and then ultimately say, "I see you—the good, the bad, the painful—and I choose all of you. Even when it doesn't feel good—and even when I may desire something else—I still commit to choosing you." The whole thing is mind-boggling to me. With this one yes, a person commits to a million tiny and big nos for hopefully decades to come. It's the ultimate practice of restraint. Yet only within this chosen restraint is there the possibility for a depth and intimacy that little else in the human experience can rival.

Real intimacy isn't accidental; it's intentional. Kiersten White emphasized this in *The Chaos of Stars*: "I didn't fall in love with you. I walked into love with you, with my eyes wide open, choosing to take every step along the way."[3]

There's something about the power of choice and the practice of restraint that distinguishes humanity from animals. And if we pause to think about it, I think we all know it.

I realized something that night at the bar. I took a living, breathing, multidimensional person and flattened him to a one-dimensional object who in that moment existed only for my pleasure.

When it doesn't matter who they are or what their name is, as long as they give us what we want in that moment, intimacy becomes a transaction, and we reduce a person to an object. We make them a little less human. When we make another person less human, we make ourselves less human too.[4] And that's not freedom; it's bondage.

I WANT WHAT I WANT

I live in New York City. It truly is the city that never sleeps. Literally at any hour of any day, I can open an app on my phone and order any type of food I want and have it delivered to my doorstep in under an hour, piping hot. Some of the longest minutes of my day are when I'm waiting for my food to arrive. As much as it pains me to admit, I too can be quite the entitled millennial. Whether it's food delivery, fitness hacks, or get-rich-overnight formulas, we eat it all up! Culture conditions us to expect and feel entitled to instant gratification. We want what we want when we want it, and we want it hand-delivered to perfection, like, yesterday. From one-night stands to casual sex to hookup apps, it's easy to see how the need for instant gratification shows up in romance, especially when it comes to the physical. It has even showed up in my life in the most unexpected moments.

I met a cute guy at the gym once. He seemed like a normal, kind person, so when he asked me out, I accepted. We had a nice dinner at his place, talked for hours, and toward the end of the night, he pulled me close for a kiss. It all felt so romantic, but things quickly unraveled.

I kid you not, within sixty seconds of our first kiss, he had somehow maneuvered out of all his clothes. I mean, the guy deserved an award for how quickly he could take his clothes off; it was quite the party trick. He then announced he was ready to have sex with me. The whole display felt so absurd that I honestly was trying not to laugh as I told him a kind but firm no. Then, as if I were a business deal he was trying to land, he started doing this negotiation dance with me. My no remained the same. Once he finally caught on that my no did indeed mean no, he claimed he had a stomachache and that he was tired. Lord, have mercy, I couldn't get out of there fast enough.

As I got in the taxi to go home, I felt like I had whiplash. What in the world just happened? And how did it all happen so fast? This person I had spent only a few hours with somehow felt entitled to my body. Why? Because he wanted what he wanted when he wanted it, and I was his perceived pathway to get there. I couldn't help but wonder how many women he had done that to and, based on his shock at my refusal, how many women that move had actually worked on. Even though I stood my ground and could objectively see what was happening, in those final minutes with him, I felt so small and objectified.

Instant gratification teaches us not only that we deserve to have what we want whenever we want it but also that what we want in the moment is the most important thing. It fosters a spirit of self-centeredness and even manipulation and treats humans as objects in a chess game.

OBJECTS TO BE CONSUMED

A few years ago, I complained to one of my pastors that the small group I had just joined was surface level. I couldn't bear one more prayer request about someone's aunt's sister's nephew's pet gerbil. My poor pastor, who had a thousand better things to do than listen to me complain about people not living up to my vulnerability standards, listened patiently. Then like my very own Yoda, he offered me this little nugget: true intimacy can't be rushed. That hit me in the gut. Truth has a way of doing that. He was right. There's nothing instant about developing the bonds of trust. It takes patience, humility, and most of all, time. It was a humbling moment.

Out of a thirst for love and connection, I have put a demand for vulnerability on my relationships for most of my life. I have so badly wanted to feel intimacy with another person that often even before holding hands, I'd find myself diving into the deep end, emotionally and spiritually skinny-dipping with a guy I barely knew. Repeatedly, I'd lead with my deepest moments of heartache, from my personal struggles to the drama and dysfunction of my family story. I was so afraid of being abandoned and rejected that my subconscious strategy was to put all my crap out there from the start, before things became too involved. On top of that, as with many Christian girls, I also wanted to know from night one whether he saw this thing going toward marriage. I didn't want to waste my time, which is fair, but the more I've thought about it, the more I don't believe there is such a thing as wasted time. Each moment, interaction, and circumstance is an opportunity to grow if we choose it to be. Plus, how are you supposed to know if you want to marry someone if you've hardly spent any time with them?

No wonder so many of my dating relationships were over before they began. Beneath all these subliminal hidden agendas, I was strategizing to get answers my heart longed for most: *Am I worthy? Will you love me? Will you stick around for me?* In my quest, all I really thought about was how I was going to get what I wanted. And that's not love; it's manipulation.

Have you ever wondered why many of us want that "instant spark" on a first date? That moment when you know he's the one? Could it be because we want to bypass the work and time it takes to develop a real relationship and connection? And have you ever noticed that even though we all want that moment, quick starts often lead to quick finishes?

Only through a lot of heartache and disappointment, I've found, like my pastor told me all those years ago, there really is no shortcut to intimacy. Instant gratification may give me on-demand pad Thai at one thirty in the morning and some momentary satisfaction, but we can't treat humans like objects or food to be consumed. And let's be real, instant gratification almost always overpromises and underdelivers. But because we're so hungry for connection, like the guy from the gym, we jump the gun and get naked prematurely, whether spiritually, emotionally, or physically. It may feel like intimacy, but it's a counterfeit, and without any solid foundation or roots, when the slightest breeze comes along, the relationship, the connection—it all falls apart.

TAKE IT FURTHER

1. What are some problems you have experienced with instant gratification?
2. How would you describe the cultural narrative you hear surrounding your sexual desire?
3. In what ways have you sought to rush intimacy in your life? What cost(s) have you paid for this?

Chapter Seven

A REAL-LIFE PRUDE UNICORN

THE MYTH THAT YOU NEED TO SHUT DOWN YOUR DESIRE

Why, when God's world is so big,
did you fall asleep in a prison
of all places?

—*Jalaluddin Rumi*

If one side of the pendulum shouts, "I am my desire," then the other side is screaming, "Eww, gross . . . turn it off!" Enter, the church.

To my non-Christian friends, I'm like a real-life prude unicorn prancing in a field of four-leaf clovers. A thirtysomething virgin? "Isn't that a movie?" people will say. But when it comes to the church, I've often felt like I lived on the outskirts. I've been the edgy one in Christian circles who doesn't accept things at face value, always asking questions and talking about all this sex stuff.

I'm a thirty-five-year-old virgin, for crying out loud, living in New York City. Even still, I was told by a prominent person in the Christian world that my story was "too racy" for the church.

I needed to tame things down a bit. Or better yet, share only from the perspective that I was ashamed of my past. The notion that my dating life is scandalous is almost laughable. *Almost* being the key word here. It'd be funny if it wasn't so personally and sexually frustrating. Jesus, take the wheel.

What is the deal with Christian culture, though?

Why are we so afraid of sex?

Why is talking about anything sex related so taboo and shame inducing?

What messages do we receive from the church about who we are in regard to our sexuality and desire?

I'm so glad you asked.

SHUT IT *DOWN*

A friend of mine was struggling with whether she wanted to marry her boyfriend. I had seen firsthand how much this guy loved her. He checked off all the boxes: loved God, had a job, and absolutely adored her. He even moved cross-country to pursue her. But as I sat on her bed and listened as she processed through her relationship, I noticed it wasn't what she said about him that gave me cause for concern; it was what she didn't say. Here we were talking about whether she wanted to marry the guy, and not once had she made any sort of comment about whether she was physically, romantically, or sexually attracted to him. Not being one to shy away from an elephant in the room, I asked her point-blank if she was.

She thought about it for a minute before sharing a hesitant, "Mm-hmm." (Pro tip: If you have to think about whether you're attracted to the person you're dating, you're probably not.) I pushed further: Did she want to have sex with him? You would've thought I asked if she had ever considered murdering him. Her eyes about popped out of her head as she threw a pillow my way, saying, "Ewww! No, I haven't thought about that. Gross, Kat!"

Say what? She was seriously considering marrying this guy, and she had never even thought about whether she desired him sexually. My question alone felt gross and dirty.

She sat there squirming like there were bugs crawling all over her skin. But if we don't want to have sex with our spouses, aren't we just roommates? And if we're not sexually attracted to the person we're dating, or the thought of being physically intimate with them grosses us out, then doesn't that mean we're just buddies? If you never feel turned on and never want to pounce on the person you're dating, then that's something to be curious about. Attraction is part of the human experience, and to feel sexually attracted to the person you're with is good, healthy, and normal!

Merely thinking about her sexual desire was scandalous to my friend. So she shut it down. I was only able to spot my friend's shame because I too have experienced it. Have you?

As I became more involved in church culture in high school and college, the more I realized that talking about sex was taboo. It felt inappropriate at best and wasn't something good Christian girls thought or talked about unless one of us was engaged and about to get married. More so, sex and desire were definitely not things you talked about in mixed company. The messages below the surface that I internalized were things like: sexual desire is shameful, it's something that belongs only within marriage, sex is taboo, and pleasure is embarrassing. So because I wanted to be a good Christian girl, I learned to keep quiet, stay appropriate, stuff my desire into a dark corner, and eventually shut it down.

PUT A BOW ON IT

Another friend of mine also grew up in church culture during the height of the purity movement. She made a promise to God to wait until marriage to have sex. She even had a purity ring she wore on her wedding ring finger to prove it. That ring remained there until a diamond engagement ring replaced it when she was twenty-six. (That's like fifty-seven in Christian years.)

Her wedding night finally came. Minutes after they undressed in front of each other for the first time, this highly anticipated moment, with all its pressure and expectations, everything fell apart. Sex was really painful for her.

She was crushed but tried not to be too worried about it since it was her first time. They tried again the next day—still painful. They tried again and again for months. The pain was incessant. Sex was excruciating, all but unbearable. None of her friends had ever talked about painful sex. She felt so much shame.

Was something wrong with her? Wasn't God supposed to bless you with incredible sex if you did things His way? And even though she was *allowed* to have sex as a married woman, why did she secretly struggle with thinking it was okay? She felt like a failure as a wife and like her body was betraying her. Slowly resentment crept into her mind and marriage. At her wits' end, she finally summoned the courage to go to the doctor. His prescription to heal her painful sex was to hurry up and get pregnant.

Sure, have a baby. That'll "open things up down there" and squash any marital issues you may be having. Because anyone who's married will tell you that if you're having trouble in your marriage, you should add a baby to the mix.

Thankfully, she didn't listen to her doctor. She decided to become the teacher she didn't have and dedicated her time to learning about her body, sex, desire, and pleasure and discovering her path toward pain-free sex. Through her journey she realized that from growing up in the church, she had attached a lot of shame to her sexual desire. All this shame and fear and compartmentalization around her sexual desire played a huge role in the physical pain she experienced in sex. Because her mind had learned to shut down her desire for all those years, her body followed suit. After several years filled with a lot of hard work and vulnerable conversations, she finally experienced pain-free sex with her husband for the first time.[1]

Recently, I was in that all-too-familiar social media rabbit hole, and a video popped up on my explore page. I watched as a middle-aged charismatic man pranced around onstage, preaching with a booming voice to a roomful of single people. His message? If you're single, you have no right to your sexuality.

This about sums up one of the most problematic narratives of the purity movement and church culture: that sexuality and desire belong only within the confines of marriage. The implication is that sexuality is and can be compartmentalized from the human experience, as though sexual desire can be wrapped in a box with a nice little bow and set on a shelf. Then one day when you get married, which may or may not ever happen, you'll pull that dusty box off the shelf, unwrap it, pull out your sexual desire, press a button, and voilà—it's turned on and ready for action. That forbidden fruit you shut down for so long, and that caused you so much angst, pain, and shame for all those years, is now totally acceptable.

In an instant you're supposed to go from a robot to a sex kitten. The pressure alone we put on this moment sets us up for further failure. If you've never ridden a bike before, you definitely won't be ready for the Tour de France on day one of training. As my friend experienced in the first few years of her marriage, our sexual desire is not a switch to be turned on and off.

TWO SIDES OF THE SAME COIN

Over the years, in hushed conversations, I have had friend after friend share with me how much she is struggling to have sex with her husband because she can't shake the mentality that it is wrong or bad or dirty. From my own personal experiences as a single woman in the church to the thousands of emails I've received from Christian women from all over the world, I know these aren't isolated experiences.

Now, in no way, shape, or form do I want to demonize the church, or culture, for that matter. I really do want to believe that many of these subtle and implicit messages are unintentional. But sometimes good intentions fall incredibly short. If we want to heal and see renewal, we must acknowledge the brokenness and its impact on people.

The back door of the church becomes wider and wider as thousands upon thousands of young people become fed up with the guilt and sexual shame they've experienced in religious circles. Disillusioned with this whole sexual narrative, and tired of feeling like failures, many people are leaving the church and Christianity altogether.

On the other hand, many Christians are having sex outside of marriage, or living with their significant other, or living a more promiscuous lifestyle, but out of shame and fear of judgment keep it hidden from their church communities.

Instead of creating a culture of honesty, we too often have a culture of hiding behind vague pleasantries. Recently, a well-known married pastor made a public statement admitting to an inappropriate relationship. What does that even mean? The statement itself couldn't have been more unclear. It was technically honest but didn't offer any real vulnerability. Outside of occasionally talking about porn, the church lacks authenticity when it comes to talking about sexuality and desire from the pulpit. This has created a culture of shame and secrets.

I wonder if this culture is why many pastors and leaders in the Western evangelical church have fallen like flies into pornography, affairs, and sexual scandal. The situation is like a pressure cooker. Eventually something is going to come out sideways.

The sexual shame that pervades church culture is as undeniable as the humidity on a hot, swampy, summer day in Houston, Texas. There's no escaping it. And shame has an agenda: to keep us stuck, compartmentalized, shut down, hidden, and isolated from God, ourselves, and others. When we shut down part of us, we shut down all of us, once again making ourselves a little less human.

As a result, we have a generation of people in the church who walk around as if they're asexual beings, following the rules while disassociating from their bodies and sexual desire.

On the surface it may seem like the opposing sides of the sexual desire pendulum couldn't be farther apart from each other. But as we look closer, we find they might not be as different as we thought.

Culture outright owns it, with the message you are your desire. In essence, your sexual desire steers the ship because it's the core of who you are. So, culturally, we worship sex. We're constantly sold the message to do what feels good in the moment at every turn, because—as every good marketer knows—sex sells.

The church, on the other hand, tries to do anything to get our minds off sex and desire, essentially screaming, *Shut it down!* This always reminds me of the scene in the movie *Mean Girls* where Coach Carr is teaching the sex ed class. He barks at a humiliated group of high school students in the gymnasium, "Don't touch each other. You will get chlamydia and die."[2] Clearly, this shut-it-down message is not working for us.

If I say, "Don't think about a purple hippo right now," what are you going to think about? A purple hippo. It's one of the oldest tricks in the book. By trying so hard not to make sexual desire a thing, the church has made it *the* thing. When this happens, subtly, sexual desire, not Jesus, becomes the center of the message. Inadvertently, as culture does, the church too worships sex.

Instead of the church and popular culture being on opposite extremes of the sexual narrative, it would seem we have two sides of the same coin. Both say, "You are your desire"—but with different PR.

Something deep down inside me knows it can't be true that I am my desire. But as much as we aren't our desire, as culture suggests, on the flip side, we aren't the absence of it either. Both sides massively miss the mark of what it means to be human.

There has to be another way.

TAKE IT FURTHER

1. What are some of the messages you've internalized from the church in regard to your sexual desire?
2. How have these internalized messages shaped your view of yourself?
3. If we aren't what culture says, "You are your desire," and shouldn't do what the church says, "Shut it down," then what role does sexual desire play in our lives?

Chapter Eight

STEPPING INTO THE GRAY

WHO AM I?

The most damaging phrase in the language is
"We've always done it this way!"
—*Grace Hopper*

When Jesus burst onto the scene, He made quite the commotion. When He saw injustice and spiritual manipulation in the church, He flipped over tables and yelled at the instigators.[1] He invited Himself to dinner at the house of one of the most hated men in town.[2] He associated with women, children, and the most ostracized people in culture. He constantly challenged the way things were, and He was gaining traction and influence. To say the least, the religious people were not happy with Him. They were always scheming to catch Jesus off guard.

One day in the middle of Jesus's teaching outside the temple, the religious leaders forced their way through the crowds and threw a woman at Jesus's feet.[3] She had been caught in the middle of having an affair, and they challenged Jesus to condemn her and stone her to death. Since she was caught in the act, obviously she wasn't alone when they found her. The fact that they didn't bring the man to Jesus for condemnation speaks volumes about the cultural norm that the religious adhered to:

women had no rights or voice and were always to blame. The highest punishment for adultery was death. In their mind, they were simply upholding the law and wanted to test Jesus to see what He'd do.

Now, imagine if this were you. First there's the trauma and humiliation of being caught in an affair, then of being dragged through town exposed in front of everyone you know. People stop and stare at you. Each step you take, more people become awakened to your shame. And then you're thrown into the middle of a church gathering and told you deserve to die because of your mistake. The weight of the shame is so heavy that you can't even lift your eyes from the ground. You hear the voices of condemnation and see feet shuffling around you. Then, all at once, silence.

Through the blur of your salty tears, you see this Jesus guy kneeling down beside you. He's writing something in the dirt. Your eyes meet His for a moment, and your heart stops. He looks at you not with eyes of judgment but with love and compassion.

Who is this man?

He then stands up and responds to the religious, saying, "Let any one of you who is without sin be the first to throw a stone at her."[4] Mystified by Jesus's response, and unable to cast judgment, the arrogant reluctantly walk away one by one until it's just you and Jesus in the middle of the crowd.

Once again Jesus finds your eyes. This time He says, "Woman, where are they? Has no one condemned you?"[5] You shake your head and whisper a no. "Neither do I. Go and sin no more," He says.[6]

Culturally speaking, because she was a woman, the woman caught in adultery had no legal rights. When it came to religion, she was a sinner who deserved death. Both extremes stripped her of her humanity and produced shame and humiliation. But then there's Jesus. He didn't dismiss the affair or pretend it wasn't there. But He led with relationship and empathy. In her darkest hour, He offered her acceptance and fought for her dignity. He restored her humanity.

Everything about this scene was scandalous. It takes my breath away.

ANOTHER WAY

Jesus blazing past the cultural and religious norms of his day wasn't a one-time thing. Jesus was constantly flipping the script, unafraid to step into the mess of humanity. In the Sermon on the Mount, Jesus said over and over again, "You have heard that it was said . . . but I tell you . . ."[7] With nuance and grace, Jesus was always stepping into the gray.

And isn't that what faith is? Seeing and experiencing the black-and-white reality of the way things are and then making a choice to step into the unseen—a more ultimate version of reality?

One of my college professors made us memorize his definition of faith. We had a pop quiz at the beginning of every single class for the entire semester. I'd tear out a sheet of notebook paper from my journal, scribble my name in the top left corner, and write down his definition: "Faith is choosing to believe the Bible is true regardless of circumstances, emotions, or societal trends."[8] I couldn't forget it if I tried.

Faith is outside the here and now; it's a deep-rooted confidence that what we see isn't always real or true. It's the belief in possibility, that outside the way things are, there could be another way.

When I think about Jesus—who He was; how He lived and interacted with people; how He loved women, children, the sick, the poor, the disadvantaged and outliers of society; how unafraid He was to ruffle the feathers of the religious elite and challenge the systems in place; and how willing He was to step into the gray spaces of people's lives—I can't help but think of where we are today in this conversation around sex and desire. I see culture giving us one set of rules to live by, the church giving another, both trying to reduce humanity to black-and-white formulas and ways of being. I wonder what Jesus thinks about it all. In the chasm between the two extremes, I believe there is another way.

And that way is the way of Jesus.

THE SPACE BETWEEN

At first there was nothing. Just void and darkness. The Spirit of God hovered over the expanse of the universe. In true God fashion, He didn't seem to be in a rush. It was almost as if God was waiting for just the right moment to burst forth with endless possibility and creativity, already showing us that He wasn't some flippant being but a thoughtful and patient God.

Then, out of the nothingness, God spoke. With an exhale, He breathed light into being. There was evening and morning. At the end of that first day, God saw what He had made and said that it was good. We see that when God collides with darkness, He doesn't see despair, but grounds that are ripe for new life.

A rhythm begins to unfold: God speaks; it is so; it is good. When God says something, it actually happens. Every single time. This cadence continues, one day building on the next as He creates stars and black holes, mountains and sea horses, tectonic plates and ants, oxygen and kiwis. God breathes life, vibrant color, and diversity into being. And all of it—from day to night, from land to sea, from trees to animals—is good. There's all this buildup until finally there's one last thing that needs to be created: humans—the climax of the creation story.

Whereas the church seems to shy away from talking about sex, desire, and sexuality, right out of the gate in the first chapter of the Bible, God leads with a rhythm, cadence, buildup, and climax that sounds, dare I say, almost . . . orgasmic.*

He doesn't seem to be embarrassed at all about the whole thing. Shocking, isn't it?

When God creates humanity, He shifts gears and does something different. He says, "Let us make human beings in our image, to be like us."[9] The *us* and *our* in this verse reference the Father, Son, and Spirit creating new life together in holy collaboration and intimate relationship.

Unique from every other aspect of creation, humans were created in God's likeness. This doesn't mean humans are God; that's pantheism. It means we are made in the image of God. Like little mirrors, we reflect our Creator. It's like seeing a child who is a walking replica of her father, not only the physical traits but also her mannerisms and characteristics—it's something in her very essence that you can't quite put your finger on.

Each time we inhale and exhale, the divine God-spark pulses through our veins an inherent worth, value, enoughness, dignity, beauty, and creativity. We don't do anything to earn this identity or make it truer; it simply is. Something about our existence alone, reflects the glory of God and His creativity. We look like our Father; the God-image is in us. The Latin phrase for this is *imago Dei*.

There's something distinct about being human, and God made it this way. My identity begins with and is defined by being made in the image of God. I am a child of God—that's

---

* I know. I know. This might feel offensive or like a vast reach for some. It did for me too. If you want to dive more into this idea of our spirituality being connected to our sexuality and how God weaves these together, a few books I'd recommend are *The Mingling of Souls* by Matt Chandler, *Divine Sex* by Jonathan Grant, *Redeeming Sex* by Debra Hirsch, *Theology of the Body for Beginners* by Christopher West, and *Sex God* by Rob Bell. This list is by no means comprehensive, and by sharing them with you I'm not saying I agree with every point, but it's a great start to dive deeper into the topic of God and sexuality.

who I am. This is the core and foundation of what it means to be human. And that must be the starting point of any conversation involving sexual desire, sexuality, or anything, for that matter. My sexual desire isn't driving the ship; my imago Dei-ness is.

The fundamental truth that I am a child of God is where the space between the culture's and the church's extremes of the sexual narrative begins. And it's also what differentiates the way of Jesus from a set of dos and don'ts when it comes to sex and desire.

I am not my desire, nor am I the absence of it. I am imago Dei. The conversation around sexuality and desire shifts when the access point starts with God, the Creator of our created selves, not with sex.

TAKE IT FURTHER

1. If Jesus scandalously and provocatively fought for the dignity of women in a time when women had no voice or rights in church or culture, what things do you think He would fight for today?
2. Have you ever considered that the creation story might have an erotic rhythm or language? What thoughts are stirred when you consider that?
3. How and in what ways do you think the conversation around sexuality shifts when we change the access point to being a child of God as opposed to either being your desire or the absence of it?

Chapter 9

TWO SIDES OF THE SAME COIN

YOUR SEXUALITY ISN'T BAD; IT'S GOD DESIGNED

Generally what is more important than
getting watertight answers is learning
to ask the right questions.

—*Madeline L'Engle*

As important as acknowledging what God says is noticing what He doesn't say. God didn't say only the human mind was good or our spirituality or just our hands and feet. The Genesis 1 text says that God saw and took into account all he created, and, "all of it was *very* good."[1] Instead of compartmentalizing, God created humans holistically.

Pastor Matt Chandler puts it this way: "When God shaped the man, he gave the man a penis. It wasn't the Devil who did that. God didn't mold most of the man and then let Satan add his own touch. Neither did Satan sneak in and alter God's good creation."[2] When talking about God creating woman, Chandler says, "And as he shaped the woman differently, he gave her larger breasts, rounder hips, and a vagina. He filled the woman with a different hormone, estrogen. The woman's body wasn't the Devil's idea; it was all God's doing."[3] God isn't like, "Oh crap, that's what happens when a guy gets turned on?" Just as He created our bodies, minds, and spirits, He also created our desire. He's not embarrassed or shocked when we get turned on, feel attraction, or long for physical intimacy.

Now, our sexuality is not the whole of who we are, but it is inextricably intertwined with what it means to be human. It's part of the God-image in us, which means that something about our desire reflects aspects of the character of God and who He is. Therefore, our sexual desire isn't taboo, bad, or shameful. God designed it, which means it's very good. And what God calls good is good. At some point we chose to begin the story about who we are from chapter 3 of Genesis, the fall of humanity, but that's not where the God-story begins.

So what does all this mean practically? Don't worry, we're getting there.

HELLO, ORGASM!

Years ago writer Bruce Marshall wrote, "The man who rings the bell at the brothel, is unconsciously looking for God."[4] Is that true? Underneath it all, are we really looking for God?

Obviously, there's the physical draw of pleasure and satisfaction. Hello, orgasm! And being skin to skin with someone feels heavenly. But stirring below the surface is something deeper. When I think about my longing for sex, I think about how I want to feel and express love, intimacy, acceptance, trust, vulnerability, unity, and connection. I want to be able to give and receive love and to see and be fully seen in a space that feels safe and supportive. Ultimately, I want to be naked and unashamed.

What are you looking for in sex?

What exactly are you hoping to find?

Why do we all so badly want to have it?

Now, let's zoom out for a minute. Whether in sex, friendship, romance, at work, the gym, or on social media, aren't we all searching to feel loved, known, understood, seen, worthy, and supported? Don't we want to feel acknowledged for our strengths, dignity, and beauty but also, and perhaps even more so, accepted in our failures and imperfections? Even when we take sex off the table, it seems as though our fundamental desires remain the same.

We're trained to think of sexuality only as it pertains to our genitals, but there's a big difference between sexual desire and the desire for sex itself. In writing of how stunted male and female dynamics are when we treat sexual desire and desire for sex as one and the same, scholar James Olthuis notices, "We are haunted by the idea, the common currency in our society, that being close always leads to the bedroom. That idea is simple, unadulterated nonsense."[5]

One of the most transformative books I've read on sexuality and spirituality is *Redeeming Sex* by church leader Debra Hirsch. From the get-go, she clearly defines sexuality "as the deep desire and longing that drives us beyond ourselves in an attempt to connect with, to understand, that which is other than ourselves. . . . It is a longing to know and be known by other people (on physical, emotional, psychological and spiritual levels)."[6]

Hirsch is saying that our sexuality is the thing inside all of us that nudges us to get outside ourselves and into relationship with others. This means we can't talk about our sexual desire and sexuality without also talking about a wide range of relationships, from friendship to family, peers, and communities. Hirsch also introduced me to Christian theologian Marva Dawn, who identifies the terms "social sexuality" and "genital sexuality" in her book *Sexual Character*.[7] Dawn explains social sexuality as the macro version of sexuality, what Hirsch describes as the human desire to connect with and be in relationship with other people, while genital sexuality obviously has to do with physical intimacy, getting naked, and sex.[8]

So if sexuality were a novel, sex and physical intimacy would be just one chapter.

THE LONGING UNDERNEATH OUR LONGING

The psalmist cries out, "As the deer *pants* for streams of water, so my soul pants for you."[9] And again, "I thirst for you, my whole being *longs* for you. . . . Your love is better than life. . . . On my bed I *remember* you; I think of you through the watches of the night . . . I *cling* to you.[10] Talk about hot and heavy, passionate language: I *pant*, I *thirst*, I *long*, I *remember*, I *cling*. It reminds me of the feeling of coming home after a date with a guy I'm crazy about. The whole night I can barely sleep because I'm so giddy. I lie there in bed replaying the night, imagining what our next date will be like. It's intoxicating and all consuming. The psalmist, however, isn't talking about a woman he is pining after but rather his relationship with God.

When was the last time you cried out to God with such visceral language because your longing for Him was so strong?

Hirsch defines spirituality "as a vast longing that drives us beyond ourselves in an attempt to connect with, to probe and to understand our world. And beyond that, it is the inner compulsion to connect with the Eternal Other, which is God. Essentially, it is *a longing to know and be known by God*. . . . This is why we are called to worship God with all that we are—body, mind and soul (Deuteronomy 6:4–9; Mark 12:29–31)."[11]

Our spirituality, then, is our core human desire to connect with the capital O Other, while sexuality is our desire to connect with the lowercase *o* other. The one is a shadow of the other: "It turns out that sexuality and spirituality are in fact two sides of the same coin. Both express a deep longing to know and be known—by God and by others."[12] Our sexuality gets us outside ourselves and into relationship with others and ultimately points us to our greater longing for God.[13] Perhaps that's what Marshall was alluding to all those years ago.

Ultimately, we can't talk about our spirituality without talking about our sexuality. Rob Bell puts it beautifully: "Sex. God. They're connected. Where the one is, you will always find the other."[14]

So is our sexuality about sex and orgasms? Yes. But we're selling ourselves short if we stop there. The physical is never just about the physical; it's infinitely more dynamic than that. Sex and desire collide in physical, emotional, intellectual, and spiritual nakedness that we all desire.

In this context, our sexuality morphs from a one-dimensional, physical act into a gem with endless facets. This is how I know there has to be a way to connect with, acknowledge, and embrace my sexuality and desire outside of sex and physical intimacy—regardless of my relationship status—in a way that honors myself, God, and others. Instead of our sexuality being confined to one physical act in the bedroom, it expands into the hall, down the stairs, and outside to pastures, fields, and rolling hills. Yes, there's still a fence out there surrounding the property, but there's way more freedom, safety, and permission to play, explore, and connect than what we may have initially thought.

I, especially as a single person, want to stop here and say that this is some *really* good news!

TAKE IT FURTHER

1. How would you describe the God-narrative of who you are?
2. What are your thoughts on the more expansive definition of sexuality? How would you define sexuality?
3. What would change for you if you believed your sexuality and desire were God designed and good?

Chapter Ten

TURNED ON

EMBRACING YOUR SEXUAL DESIRE 101

When you love a good thing for what
it is; it becomes what it should be.
—*Q. Gibson*

When we live in an all-or-nothing culture, it can feel a lot easier to put something to death than to take the time to figure out what a healthy manifestation of that something looks like. I've worked at more than one ministry where I had to sign a contract saying that as long as I worked there, I would never have a sip of alcohol. If all alcohol is bad all the time, why did Jesus turn water into wine so that His friends could keep the party going at a wedding reception?[1] Perhaps Jesus was inviting us to leave behind the black-and-white systems that make us feel safe temporarily and to step into the nuance and gray.

The opposite of drunkenness is not abstinence. There's space between not taking a sip of alcohol ever and being totally obliterated. Scripture says to eat, drink, and be merry.[2] We all have different thresholds, and it takes time, space, and grace to figure out what those are. It takes humility to allow ourselves and each other to figure out what our boundaries are.

The same principle can be applied when we enter a conversation about embracing our sexuality. There's a wide spectrum of experiences, from being completely shut down to our sexuality and desire to running around town in nothing but nipple tassels.

In the last chapter, we talked about a macro version of sexuality. Physical intimacy and sex, or genital sexuality, are ways to express our sexuality and desire, but they're not the *only* way. If it's true that our sexuality boils down to the human desire for connection, then there are a million and one ways to access and celebrate sexuality in God-honoring ways that don't involve sex or said nipple tassels.

As I unpack different ways to embrace your sexuality over the next three chapters, pretend like we're playing dress-up. I'll offer up an idea, and you can try it on. If it doesn't fit or feel good, try on something else. Before throwing something aside, be curious. Some things may not be for you; other things may feel weird because they're new. Leaving our comfort zone is often the beginning of transformation.

Also, what works for you may not work for someone else and vice versa. That's okay. Perhaps your way isn't the only way. God knows I love being right and blowing my morality police whistle. But as Jon Tyson writes, "When we read the Gospels, we find it wasn't the immoral but the self-righteous who were the biggest hindrance to the mission of Jesus in the world. I shudder when I realize how much of that judgmentalism has seeped into my own heart."[3] What do you say we leave our judgments at the door? Part of stepping into the gray with our sexuality is giving ourselves and others the permission to be on their own journey with God through these complex questions.

ACKNOWLEDGE YOUR DESIRE

Repeatedly, Scripture says that out of the overflow of our hearts, our mouths speak.[4] Our hearts not only drive our words but also propel our actions. Learning to embrace your sexuality is an inside-out job. If we deny or judge the existence of our desires and keep them in the dark, how can we ever learn to discern an honorable way to embrace them?

Shutting down your desire dismisses part of your humanity, and repression creates a pressure cooker. My pastor friend Ashley puts it like this: "In a desire to pursue what's pure and holy we've actually pushed down our desires. We've denied that they even exist. . . . We experience thoughts or temptations that we can't even admit to ourselves yet alone others, and instead of inviting in the right amount of support and accountability we try to deal with in the dark what can only be overcome in the light. That's why you see Christian leaders who are taken out by their own moral failures."[5] It's when things are trapped in the dark that they morph and get twisted.

So first things first: bring your desire to the light and acknowledge it. Why? Because God cares about your sex drive. In fact, He custom designed it just for you. It's not sinful to have desires and feel turned on. Praying away your libido is praying away part of what it means to be a human made in the image of God. You don't have to freak out when you feel it, hide it from God, or pretend it's not there.

When you feel turned on, let yourself feel the feels. If you are desiring physical intimacy, be honest with yourself about it. I long for physical touch and intimacy on the daily. Being skin to skin with a person you like and are attracted to is awesome. Acknowledge and honor the sensations that pass through your body, and thank God for them.

Next, invite God into those moments with you. What makes Jesus different from other gods is that He lived a human life.[6] Jesus was single and fully human. This means He 100 percent had a sex drive and experienced physical longing and arousal. If Jesus was able to do that and not sin, then we can learn how to do that too. As Jesus did, we can learn to honestly acknowledge what we're feeling and figure out what to do with those feelings. Finally, like Ashley said, invite safe people to walk this journey with you. When you bring hidden things into the open, you'll almost always discover you're not the only one.

ACTIVATE INTERCESSION

Next, allow your desire to activate intercession. Pastor Mark Batterson says, "Bold prayers honor God, and God honors bold prayers."[7] Be bold and specific with your desires. Pray for the spouse you may or may not have even met yet—if marriage is something you desire. Why? Because God is able to do anything.[8]

Ask God to practically show you how to connect to your sexual desire in a way that brings honor to Him, yourself, and your future. God answers prayers all the time, but sometimes our prayers are so vague that we miss the blessing.

Don't know how or what to pray about your sexuality? Start with gratitude.

EXPRESS GRATITUDE

Scripture says to enter God's presence with thanksgiving and praise.[9] Thank God for giving you sexual desire. Thank God for creating your body in such a way that it feels things. Thank God for creating pleasure.

God didn't have to create taste buds to enjoy chocolate cake, but He did. God didn't have to create humor and laughter, but He did. Have you ever seen an infant laugh after farting? It's total innocence. God didn't have to create our bodies and nerve endings to enjoy physical intimacy, but He did. Express gratitude for that. Beginning with a posture of gratitude shifts the internal landscape of our hearts and connects our spirit to hope.

DISCERN

Yes, God created our sex drive and sexual desire, but that doesn't mean that every time we feel turned on that those feelings come from a grounded place. When you feel connected to your desire, ask, "How did I get here?" Are you turned on because you've been watching porn, reading erotic novels, or watching movies and shows with explicit sex scenes? Are you feeling awakened to your desire because you just had a hot makeout? (By the way, I love a hot makeout!) Are you feeling your sex drive because it's a Tuesday afternoon and it's simply a natural human response to being alive?

What is your desire propelling your toward? Is there anything it's taking you away from? Remember, our sexuality propels us into relationship with others. Ask God to give you a picture of what it looks like to have your desire point you toward relationship with others.

So much of this process of discernment hinges upon your willingness to look inward and be honest with yourself. Get curious. What do you want to happen when you feel turned on? Does connecting to your desire make you want to have sex, masturbate, or maybe just go on a date? Sometimes when I feel my desire, it awakens my deep longing for marriage and children. Other times I feel like I want to do a really good workout or go dancing. And there's also times when I feel turned on that I really just want to experience an orgasm and being skin to skin with someone.

In the New Testament, Jesus asked a blind man what he wanted healing from, not because Jesus didn't know the guy was blind. Something powerful happens for us when we are able to articulate what we want, need, and hope for. Honesty allows us to take responsibility and ownership over our desires as opposed to feeling like a victim to our sex drive. Clarity allows us to be connected to our hearts and cling to the possibility of hope instead of shutting it down out of shame. The blind man was clear what he wanted Jesus to do for him, so when the miracle came, he knew who to thank.

For so much of my Christian life, I hid my desire out of shame. If I was honest that I wanted marriage and intimacy and sex, did that mean I wasn't content in my relationship with God? Wasn't God supposed to be enough for me? Over time I've found that the answer to the problem with this narrative is in the Bible. Within the first few pages, God says it's not good for humans to be alone.[10] God knew we needed human relationships to flourish. We also experience God in profound ways when we experience the God-image in each other. So what is it that you desire?

I've also hid behind vagueness as a self-preservation strategy. If I didn't get my hopes up, that would protect me from disappointment if I didn't get the thing I wanted. But here's the thing: even when I'm not honest with myself, the hope and expectation is still there. Little else rivals the pain of disappointment. But part of being open to love is risking the possibility of pain, rejection, heartache, and disappointment. We have to be open to one to be open to the other.

And then there's weird things people say: "It'll happen when you least expect it" or "It'll happen when you're finally content." If I had a nickel for every time someone told me this, I'd have at least twenty-seven dollars. At least. We walk around pretending we're content and pretending we're not hoping for a relationship, thinking if we play things just right, we'll trick God into giving us a partner. As if that's how God works. But here's what's true: people meet their significant others every single day. Sometimes it's by total surprise, and other times it's on the 143rd online date. The bigger reality is this: God already knows the deepest desires of our hearts. The psalmist cried out that before a word leaves our lips, God knows it fully.[11] Pretending we don't want something in order to get the thing we say we don't want is like being the girl who tells her boyfriend she's *fine* when he asks her what's wrong and then walks away slamming cabinets. It's a fear-based strategy and also highly passive-aggressive.

Imagine if the blind man said he wanted his sight and Jesus said no. How painful that would have been. And yet. Even with the possibility of disappointment, the blind man courageously chose hope as he verbalized exactly what he wanted Jesus to do for him. The blind man knew that his heart and his deepest longings were safe with Jesus.

Ultimately, if we want to discern our sexual desire, we have to be clear about what it is we're really longing for. If we want to be clear, we have to be courageously honest with ourselves, God, and trusted others. Clarity lifts the fog surrounding our desires and circumstances and creates the space to discern what our next step can be. It allows us to take responsibility and ownership over what it is that we want.

Can you give yourself the permission to simply notice what's coming up for you without judging or shaming yourself for what you want? When you're able to be honest and identify specifically what desires you're wanting, then you're able to make a decision from a holistic place as to how you want to move forward.

TALK IT OUT

A few years ago, I was on a friend's podcast.[12] She asked me about being single in my thirties in New York City and not having sex. My response: it's freaking hard. Anyone who says it isn't is a liar. Navigating singleness in today's culture with all the swipe rights and swipe lefts and ghosting and sliding into those DMs can be a real struggle fest.

In less than a month after that episode went live, I received thousands of emails from women all over the world saying they had no idea they were allowed to admit out loud that they loved God, that they wanted to have sex, and that the whole in-between period was hard.

Sometimes vulnerability feels like being the friend that wants to go skinny dipping. Deep down the others want to do it too, but someone has to make the first move. Trust me, your friends are dying to talk about this stuff; it just takes the courage of one person being willing to take that initial plunge.

Talk with your people about your desire—and by that I'm not encouraging you to go directly to social media to share your experience with strangers on the internet. By the time of that podcast interview, I had been processing this stuff with my community for over five years. My mentor once told me to share from a scar, not a scab. Instead of making your process a teaching point for strangers on the internet, walk it out with real people in real time. Talking about my sexuality has normalized my desire and in that brought such healing and freedom. The chains of shame are unlocked when we bring hidden things into the light. Who in your life is safe and can walk with you and process this conversation with you?

You didn't think the only way I was going to tell you to embrace your sexuality was to pray about it, did you? We're about to get to the good stuff; it's time to get practical.

TAKE IT FURTHER

1. Spend some time journaling and praying. Ask God to speak to you about your sexual desire.
2. Up until now, how have you treated your sexual desire? Have you shut it down? How can you move forward in acknowledging, honoring, and accepting it? One thing you can do is to write a letter to your sexual desire. Thank God for it, accept it, bless it, and pray for it.
3. If you feel any shame about your desire, be honest with God about it. God wants to know you, and your heart is completely and utterly safe with Him!

PHASE THREE

The Practical

Chapter Eleven

SEXUAL HEALING

SENSUALITY AND THE PRACTICE OF PRESENCE

The practice of staying present will heal you. Obsessing about how the future will turn out creates anxiety. Replaying broken scenarios from the past causes anger or sadness. Stay here, in this moment.

—*S. McNutt*

Have you ever seen a toddler play in a bed of green grass? They're letting it run between their fingers, pulling it out of the ground, touching the cool blades, smelling and studying it like it's the most fascinating thing they've ever seen. Let's be real: at some point they're going to put it in their mouth. Nothing else matters outside of getting to know grass. They're completely mesmerized.[1]

Sensual. The word itself feels so . . . sensual? In reality, it has less to do with sexy lingerie and candles dripping wax, and way more to do with being alive to our senses and in the moment. Sensuality is simply the art of being present. It's being connected to and present to your senses.

If you want to know how to practice presence, go spend

an afternoon with a baby. Babies are sensuality experts—they experience life through what they see, hear, smell, touch, and taste. The child playing in the grass is 100 percent present and alive to their senses.

Did you know the top libido killers are responsibility, stress, and lack of sleep? So when that bill needs to be paid and dishes are stacked up in the sink, good luck getting in the mood. What makes a powerful sexual experience is the ability, or discipline, really, to be fully immersed in the moment at hand, connected to yourself and the person you are with. The last time I checked, we're not present people. Whether it's our phones, social media, Netflix, or checking our email a thousand times a day, we allow ourselves to be constantly bombarded with distractions. We are multitaskers to a fault, and our divided attention keeps us from being present to the here and now.

When was the last time you watched a show without checking your phone at least once? When was the last time you were so present in an experience that nothing else mattered outside of being fully alive to the moment at hand? If you're distracted in every area of your life, what makes you think you won't be distracted in the bedroom? Strengthening the muscle of sensuality is a discipline that will not only transform your life and relationships—it's also one of the best ways to connect with your sexuality and desire.

Light some candles, turn on an oil diffuser, throw on an outfit you feel like a million bucks in, put on some music, and have a dance party in your bedroom. Who cares if you have no rhythm? Just go with it. Notice what the fabric feels like on your skin. What does your room smell like? How does it feel to move your body?

Host a dinner party and have everyone leave their phones in a bowl in the other room so everyone can be present. Notice how the experience changes when there are no distractions.

Try not checking your email or social media for the first and last hour of each day.

You could read a book, or just be present to the feelings of waking up, making a cup of coffee, and connecting to your surroundings.

Go watch a sunset. Sit in the quiet and notice the colors. What does it look like? What does it feel like? What does it sound and taste like?

Finally, take your earbuds out, and put your phone away! Anytime we have a split second of boredom or transition, we pull out our phones. Whether you're in line at the grocery store, in a cab, or at the dentist office, what if you chose to keep your phone tucked away and stay present? Who knows what God could have for you in that moment? Notice what happens in your body and mind the moment you feel the need to check your phone, but choose not to.

SEX MAKES BABIES (DUH)

A few summers ago, I went to my first and last music festival with my brother and sister. It rained almost the entire day, it was freezing cold, my brother and I both had our cell phones stolen, and we got separated from our sister for hours with no way of reaching her. Sopping wet and totally defeated, we started heading for the subway. But then we heard Brandon Flowers, lead singer of The Killers, belt the first line to "Mr. Brightside." We instantly turned around and sprinted back through the soggy grounds to the stage. I had been holding my pee for so long because it was so cold and rainy that as soon as we started running to the stage, I legit peed myself. We stayed for the entire show, piss shorts and all, and sang and danced at the top of our lungs with a sea of people, the Manhattan skyline lighting up the night.

There's something transcendent about concerts. You have thousands of people coming together who have different values, belief systems, worldviews, and political leanings. But for a few hours, none of that matters. Everyone is singing, dancing, connecting; it's total unity. All because a few people got together and decided to create something together and put it out in the world.

Art and creativity aren't about whether you can paint or sing a high note; they're about making something new in community. Doing so not only allows us to connect to the heart of God but also creates powerful bridges of unity and human connection.

Sex makes babies; it's the ultimate form of collaboration. It's passion, adventure, intimacy, vulnerability, and creativity expressed. Zooming out, we can use that same principle when it comes to connecting with and expressing our sexuality. We can do that by diving into diverse, outward-focused communities and creating new things together.

When you feel turned on, instead of shutting down that arousal or shaming yourself, embrace it. Use that energy and make something with it. You can have an eroticism for life, a vigor, a passion, a zeal within you that when channeled can create tidal waves of connection with the world around you. What lights you up? Travel? Sports? Finance? Reading? Science? Podcasts? Accounting? Graphic design? Grab some people, brainstorm, and make it happen. The possibilities are endless.

TREAT YO'SELF

After seven years of not going on a single date, I met a guy backstage at New York Fashion Week. I thought he was just about the hottest thing ever and almost died when he kissed me in the shadows of a dark East Village dive bar. We started dating, if that's what you want to call it. He would wait until the last minute to make plans with me, then show up hours late or not at all. When he did show, he was aloof and constantly on his phone. Insecure and starved for attention, I made every excuse in the book to justify his behavior.

I heard once that people are trained to detect counterfeit money not by spending their days looking at fake money but by studying in as much detail as possible what the real thing looks, feels, sounds, and smells like. Maybe tastes like too, but I'm not 100 percent sure about that. Those tiny unnoticeable details that no one else picks up on? They know them like the back of their hand. By the time a counterfeit comes across the table, they can spot it a mile away.

I couldn't discern the real thing from the counterfeit because I forgot what it looked and felt like to be romanced. So I started to ask myself some questions. How did I want to be treated? If I didn't want last-minute texts like "U up?" then how did I want to be communicated with? What sort of dates felt fun and exciting? Then I started to be intentional about doing those activities with and for myself. I even block off a date night on my calendar every week that I protect and honor. If a guy asks me out, then bam, I already have space open, and if not, then I use it as time to romance myself.

You don't have to wait for a date to make you feel good. Show yourself how you want to be treated. Take yourself on dates. Is there a museum exhibit you want to see? A new restaurant you've been dying to check out? Make a reservation. Get dressed up and throw on some lipstick and heels, because you are worth it, with or without an audience. And be present. Put your phone away—how rude to be on social media while you're on a date!

Get to know what you desire, treat yourself how you want to be treated, and when the time comes, you'll not only be able to distinguish between the real and the counterfeit but also know how to communicate what it is that you like. Part of embracing your desire is being able to communicate consent, aka what you do and don't like. Romance and desire go hand-in-hand. Take some time getting to know what you like and how you desire to be treated.

HEAD TO HEART

Part of shutting down our sexuality and desire is separating ourselves from our bodies. Our sexuality isn't a switch that magically gets turned on when we get married. That mindset flattens what it means to be human. It fosters disassociation between our bodies and spirits. The message we absorb is that the spirit is good and the body is bad. Unfortunately, a lot of Christians have received this message from church culture, but it's time to set the record straight. The idea that the body is secondary and even evil in relation to the more superior and elevated spirit is rooted in the belief system of Gnostic dualism stemming from ancient Greek philosophy. What makes Jesus different from other religions is that He cares about the whole person.

When we dissociate from our bodies, we tend to live in our heads. Our heads are the logical, rule-following, doing part of us. We need our heads. They help us stay alive and get things done, but our hearts are equally committed to protecting us. The heart is where we experience emotion and intuition, those gut checks when we walk into a room or situation and even though we can't quite put our finger on it, something feels off. I've put myself in countless unsafe situations with men, stayed at churches where leadership lacked integrity, and remained in toxic work environments because I've been conditioned to believe that my body is bad and my heart and emotions can't be trusted. Only in hindsight do I see how in almost every case that I sensed something was off, it actually was. My body, heart, emotions were indeed trustworthy, and if only I had been given the freedom to trust myself, I would've been protected from a lot of heartache, disfunction, and pain. I'm learning now more than ever how clearly and consistently God speaks to us through our hearts, bodies, and experiences.

But how do we even embark on a path toward reassociating with our bodies and learning to listen to and trust our hearts when we've been conditioned for so long to dissociate? As with any transformation journey, it starts by taking tiny consistent steps in a new direction; in this case toward building trust and closing the chasm between our heads and hearts. One practical way we can do this is through connecting to our breath.

In the beginning God breathed the universe into existence and breathed the breath of life into humanity. Creation is the exhale of God. When we connect to our breath, we're connecting to our Creator. We're bringing association back into our body, not just our minds.

You can connect to your breath by working out or moving your body in some way and choosing to focus on your breath. This is one reason I love vinyasa yoga. With each inhale and exhale, you move into a different posture; it's movement linked to breath. When I get stuck in my head, whether I can't stop thinking about a conflict with a friend who said the thing I wish I would've had the guts to say in person but didn't, or feeling stuck on a chapter in this book, I'll physically get up from my desk and put on some music and dance. When twirling, stomping my feet, and flailing around, I'm actively choosing to be in my body. Oddly enough there's something about taking a break from my head that often brings me the clarity I was seeking as I sat steeped in the endless loop of my thought life. This is also why many athletes say running clears their head. For those miles on the pavement, it's just you and your breath.

Another way to connect to your breath is learning to lengthen your inhales and exhales. Boxed breathing is a great option.

Imagining the four sides of a box, you simply breathe in, hold your breath, breathe out, hold your breath, each for an equal amount of time, say, four seconds. Repeat this cycle ten to twenty times. As you breathe, focus on your breath. If you notice your mind starting to wander or going back to tasks you have to accomplish, don't worry. You're human. Simply make the choice to return to your breath. If you need a thought or word to anchor your breath work, go for it. I'll often take a psalm and pull out a phrase to focus on, for example, Psalm 46:10: "Be still, and know that I am God." You can inhale *be*, exhale *still*. If you're struggling with stress or anxiety, you can extend your exhales to be longer than your inhales—for example, inhale for four seconds, hold for four, exhale for six, hold for four. When you exhale more than you inhale, you activate your parasympathetic nervous system. This takes your body from being in fight-or-flight mode to a place of rest. It's the body's way of telling your mind that you are safe and have permission to relax. By utilizing our breath, we are able to stabilize our bodies, minds, and spirits. Our breath anchors us in our bodies and actively bridges the gap between our head and heart. God designed us this way.

But what does reassociating our minds and bodies have to do with embracing our sexuality? More than you know. Jesus's invitation isn't only to know facts about Him. Transformation happens with the collision of knowledge and experience—the head and the heart. It's why the Bible says to love the Lord your God with all your heart, soul, and mind.[2] The psalmist says that God knows our names.[3] The Hebrew here implies an intimate, immersive, full-body and spirit experience of knowing. The same word for God knowing us in the Psalms is used in Genesis 4:1 when Adam "knew" Eve, aka, when they had sex.

Sex here isn't about mechanics or technique but the physical manifestation of intimately knowing someone mind, body, and spirit. Remember, sexual encounters are most fulfilling when we're able to leave the to-do lists at the door and be fully alive to the moment at hand—in other words, when we're able to go from our head to our hearts. This, again, is the practice of presence, or sensuality.

As we integrate our sexuality and desire into our lives, regardless of our relationship status, one of the most important things we have to learn is how to move from the head to the heart and learn how to practice the art of being present.

WHAT ABOUT . . . YOU KNOW . . .

Finally, we can't talk about embracing our sexuality without talking about masturbation. For many years, the word alone felt shame inducing. But shame doesn't get to have the final word. Not today. It's time to have an honest, shame-free, nuanced conversation about masturbation.

TAKE IT FURTHER

1. What is one way you can implement sensuality in your life today? Extra credit: What are three things you can do this week to practice presence?
2. Make a list of things you want to do and experience. Grab your calendar, and schedule a solo date for this month.
3. Go to a quiet place, get comfortable, pick a relaxing song, set a timer for five minutes, and practice boxed breathing. If you need an anchoring thought, "Be still, and know that I am God" is a great place to start. Inhale *be*, exhale *still*. When you're done, journal about your experience.

Chapter Twelve

MY DIRTY LITTLE SECRET

IS MASTURBATION A SIN?

The only thing wrong with being an atheist is
that there's nobody to talk to during an orgasm.
—*Author unknown*

When I was growing up, my mom normalized masturbation. She'd say things like, "Everybody plays with themselves." But something about it seemed so embarrassing—and I definitely didn't want to talk about it with *her*. Even still, I secretly did it *all the time*; it felt like my dirty little secret.

I can't tell you the exact moment I discovered it, but it was either when I felt the water jets blast in the pool or climbed the pole at recess with my legs wrapped tightly around it. I had no idea what an orgasm was; I just knew that when something rubbed between my legs at a certain pressure, something magical happened.

Years later, I became a Christian. Soon after, I learned new words like *purity*. At church, the pastors wouldn't actually say the word *masturbation* from the pulpit. They'd just sort of raise their eyebrows, cock their head to the side, and hop around the issue by saying things like *lust* or *sexual sin* or making some vague reference about looking up stuff on your computer late at night. And they'd only address the men in the room, as if men are the only ones with sexual desires. Quietly humiliated, I wondered if I was the only Christian girl who had ever touched herself. Ashamed, I quit cold turkey, assuming one day soon I'd get to have all the orgasms I wanted. (Christians from the South got married at, like, nineteen.)

Over time I continued to shut down and shame my desire until it all but burned out.

SWEET RELIEF

Fast-forward a decade, and I was still very single—no ring by spring for me. On the heels of a bad breakup, I went on my own mini version of *Eat, Pray, Love*. For the first time in my adult life, I began seeking freedom and wholeness. In therapy I was learning that if we don't heal our past, it follows us. When I began struggling with debilitating anxiety attacks, I learned that our physical bodies are speaking to us constantly about spiritual things if only we would take the time to pause and listen. Through yoga, I learned that connecting with our bodies and our breath was a sacred thing.* Through all these different avenues, I discovered we're not compartmentalized beings. We can't turn off part of us without the whole being affected.

It felt like I was waking up from a deep sleep. As I became more and more committed to living a fully integrated life, something else woke up too: my sexual desire. After years of being on lockdown—how can I put this delicately?—I was *burning with passion*.[1] But I had no idea what that meant for this area of my life as a single person who loved God.

Like coming home after a long day and taking off a suffocating bra, masturbation felt like sweet relief, and this time around I

---

* I know. You might be freaking out that I practice yoga. I have a lot to say about it, but all I'll say now is God wants to redeem all things, and that means all things. I feel peace about doing yoga as a Christian but understand it's not for everyone.

didn't feel guilty about it. Even though as a young Christian I felt like the only girl who had ever touched herself, literally everyone I talked to, from pastors to friends, had masturbated. I started to wonder if masturbation really was a sin. There were people in my life all for it, others totally against it, and others somewhere in between. I honestly could make any decision I wanted, knowing wherever I landed I'd have some sort of justification. However, I wanted to take ownership over my decisions and continue to develop a healthy sexual ethic.

For me this has meant unpacking how I got here. What did I learn about masturbation from home, church, and through my personal experience? Then I looked at my values, which are birthed out of my relationship with God. How does my faith impact how I participate, or not, in self-pleasure? Does Scripture have any wisdom to offer? What do science and research have to say? Finally, if I am a child of God, and God speaks to humanity, then what is God saying to me specifically in regard to masturbation? We can call this wisdom, discernment, intuition, our gut, or the Holy Spirit speaking to us.

In order to develop a holistic and healthy sexual ethic, we have to move through the process of deconstruction and then reconstruction before getting to the practical. This, by the way, is the framework you've been seeing throughout this entire book in action. Throughout this chapter, I hope to show you the different perspectives surrounding masturbation so you can discern for yourself what you believe and why about masturbation, and what decisions you want to make for yourself.

TRUST THE PROCESS

There is a myriad of topics that the Bible isn't necessarily clear about, like who exactly you should marry or how to date, since dating as we know it didn't exist in biblical times. Simply put, the Bible doesn't talk about masturbation explicitly. It does talk about lust and fantasizing, but I'm not convinced masturbation is always connected to lust.

Perhaps masturbation is a gray area. This doesn't mean God doesn't care about it or that there isn't wisdom that can be applied from the Scriptures. It just means there isn't a prescriptive answer for all people at all times.

When Jesus invited Peter to leave the safety of the boat to walk on the water with Him, it made no sense.[2] It defied science and logic. But Jesus wasn't afraid of bursting through the mold of our linear understanding. As long as Peter kept his eyes on Jesus and trusted Him, he was able to experience the seemingly impossible with Him. When we step into the unknown, we don't have to be afraid. We just need to keep our eyes on Jesus and trust the process—easier said than done, I know.

However, my invitation to you through these next few pages is to do just that.

THE BIG "O"

You know the explosive, all-consuming feeling that has the power to bring presidents to their knees, while it can also close the chasm between a couple, fostering unparalleled intimacy? Little else rivals the orgasm.

What exactly happens in our bodies when we orgasm? For starters, our brains release an outpouring of dopamine and oxytocin.

Dopamine is a neurotransmitter released from the reward center part of the brain associated with pleasure. It's like when kindergarteners receive gold stars for good behavior. You learn to raise your hand instead of blurting out the answer because you get rewarded for your good behavior. Soon enough, we don't even have to think about it; we just raise our hands until we're called on.[3] Your dopamine center activates when you get a "like" or comment on social media, when you eat a dessert you've been craving, or when you exercise. It's part of what contributes to a runner's high. These dopamine releases create well-grooved, bicycle-like pathways in our brains, called neuropathways, so the craving for and execution of good behaviors become second nature. The mind is always looking to identify patterns in order to automate behavior to free up the mind to focus on other things like, say, keeping us alive.

Oxytocin is known as the feel-good hormone. One of its sole purposes is to create deep attachments between people.[4] During breastfeeding, oxytocin is released in both mother and child, helping to create that impenetrable mother-child bond.[5] It also releases when we hug a friend and in that electric moment when the guy you like reaches for your hand the first time. The oxytocin released in orgasm is why some researchers now believe there is no such thing as casual sex. The bonding hormones in our bodies don't allow for it.[6]

Oxytocin and dopamine aren't just released during sex or orgasm but also when we experience sexual and emotional intimacy with another person. Because of the dopamine and oxytocin release, the more you experience sexual intimacy with a person, throughout time, the more your body craves intimacy with them. Over time and with repeated experiences with the same person, even the mere thought of them can become arousing. It's the whole "gold star" experience in action. These patterned hormonal releases help solidify a pathway created by our brains to inform our bodies with the message "this is how we get aroused." This then combines with development and strengthening of bonds prompted by the oxytocin release. In other words, it's like when raising your hand in class gives you gold stars enough times that it becomes second nature. Neurologically speaking, it would seem that God hardwired us for intimacy. I wonder if this could be the science behind what a lot of Christians refer to as *soul ties*.

When we take science and research into account, the cultural narrative that treats monogamy and marriage like a death to incredible sex doesn't seem to hold up. The long-term, committed, monogamous relationship can actually be the beginning of a journey toward the best sex of your life. Science for the mic drop!

This is exactly why pornography is so destructive. These chemicals were designed to further intimacy within relationship, not a one-dimensional fantasy. You can be in a loving relationship with your partner, yet unable to be aroused by them because you have trained your body to crave pornography.

In healthy encounters with things like food, water, and even sex, the dopamine release naturally subsides after you've had your fill and are satisfied. It's why even though you're eating the best meal of your entire life, you eventually stop eating when you're full.

However, the brain can be tricked. One of the effects of using hard drugs like cocaine is that the reward center is blocked from stopping the outpouring of dopamine. It keeps releasing more and more dopamine, which is why the high is so intense and addictive.

Research shows that pornography reacts with the brain in the exact same way. When porn is consumed, it triggers a short circuit to the reward center and fools the brain into continuing the outpouring of dopamine, thus creating the same incredibly addictive feeling of being high that hard drugs offer. Here's the catch: you're not only unable to get full; the craving for the thing that triggers the short circuit continues to increase. Like the drug addict, the porn addict is forever chasing the intensity of their initial high.[7] What got you off in the beginning won't sustain the pace of your brain's blocked reward center. This is why we see people progress from "soft" porn, like *Maxim*, to "hard" porn to child pornography.[8]

Almost every Christian man I have spoken to about masturbation—and trust me I've spoken to a lot—has told me it's nearly impossible to masturbate without using porn. To me this sentiment simply gives us a window into the severity of the porn addiction in our culture. However, from personal experience, research, and hundreds of honest conversations, I know this: it's 100 percent possible to masturbate without consuming porn.

All in all, the orgasm is incredibly powerful and can either sustain or destroy a relationship.

So what does this mean for the single woman in her sexual prime who is seeking God, abstaining from sex until marriage, and feeling all the feels? Let's keep digging.

THE HAREM WITHIN

You may know C. S. Lewis from the *Chronicles of Narnia*, his friendships with literary greats like J. R. R. Tolkien, or his famous conversion story and profound work on Christian apologetics, but he also had a lot to say about masturbation. In an essay, Lewis wrote,

> For me the real evil of masturbation would be that it takes an appetite which, in lawful use, leads the individual out of himself . . . and turns it back: sends the man back into the prison of himself, there to keep a harem of imaginary brides. And this harem, once admitted, works against his ever getting out and really uniting with a real woman. For the harem is always accessible, always subservient, calls for no sacrifices or adjustments, and can be endowed with erotic and psychological attractions which no real woman can rival. Among those shadowy brides he is always adored, always the perfect lover: no demand is made on his unselfishness, no mortification ever imposed on his vanity.

> In the end, they become merely the medium through which he increasingly adores himself. . . . After all, almost the main work of life is to come out of our selves, out of the little, dark prison we are all born in. Masturbation is to be avoided as all things are to be avoided which retard this process. The danger is that of coming to love the prison.[9]

Sex has the capacity and power to express, manifest, and create otherness. As Lewis implies, one of the real beauties of sexual desire is that it propels us toward relationship with people. It's in relationship with others that new life is created. In the most literal sense, a byproduct of sex is babies.

So if love ends on itself, is it really love? Here lies what I think to be one of the greatest risks of masturbation: it can isolate us from in-the-flesh, real-life relationships, and not just romantic ones but friendship and community too. It places us at the center of our own universe, teaching us that our pleasure is to be prioritized above all else.

There's a famous *Sex in the City* episode where sweet Charlotte discovers the magic of the Rabbit vibrator. The four girls are at brunch when Miranda talks about her latest love affair; it just so happens to be with her vibrator. Charlotte is appalled, replying, "A vibrator doesn't call you on your birthday. A vibrator doesn't send you flowers the next day, and you cannot take a vibrator to meet your mother. . . . I'm saving sex for a man I love."[10]

But a few scenes later, Charlotte finds herself with the other girls, purchasing her very own Rabbit. Pretty soon she is so taken with her new toy that she is canceling plans to go to the ballet, lying to her friends, and refusing to leave her apartment until Miranda and Carrie finally burst into her bedroom for an intervention. In defense, Charlotte pleads, "It's no big deal; it's just I'd rather stay at home with the Rabbit than deal with men."

The girls persist until Charlotte agrees to leave her apartment and hand over her vibrator. In true Carrie fashion, the scene closes with her poignant narration: "With a little help from her friends, Charlotte decided she wasn't going to settle for herself."

The reality is that anytime you bring two people together, there are wounds and baggage, and whether platonic or romantic, it's messy. This may make self-gratification an undeniably easier option, but it doesn't give us the experience of intimacy and the feeling of being known that we truly long for. With relationships there will always be the risk of pain, rejection, failure, heartache, and conflict. But there's also the potential for feeling a deep sense of love, connection, and acceptance. The reality is that cultivating authentic intimacy requires time, communication, commitment, humility, conflict, and a resolve to be outward focused.

Having roommates, I'm daily confronted with the humbling realities that I want to be right, I want to be in control, and I want things done my way . . . all the time. It's okay if I leave *my* shoes out, but if my roommate does it, she's a hoarder. The people we're closest to mirror back to us our flaws, and in that we have the opportunity to course correct. Scripture calls this iron sharpening iron.[11] Completely enamored, *the harem within* doesn't ask you if you paid the water bill; they're not concerned with your personal development. When we're surrounded by an arena of yes-men, there's no possible way to grow. There's just no way around it: relationships are as challenging as they are risky.

I recently had a conversation with a guy. He loves God and is funny, charismatic, and single. I was baffled when I found out he hadn't been snatched up—yeah, he was that attractive. Over the course of our conversation, we hit some hot topics—masturbation being one of them. He made a passing yet revealing comment. He said he would never want a girl to give him a hand job because no one would be able to do it as good as he could do it. So instead of taking the time to communicate and develop intimacy with a partner, he'd rather just do it on his own.

Now, I'm all for knowing your body—this empowers us to give informed and enthusiastic consent in our sexual encounters. But I don't want to be so good at getting myself off that it's not worth putting myself out there to be in a relationship with a real person. Could this be a reason this guy was still single?

Instead of taking the risk of investing in a relationship, we compartmentalize and settle for short-term fulfillments that are a far cry from what we really want.

In our quick-fix culture, have we gotten so good at pleasuring ourselves that the cost it takes to put ourselves out there, go through the awkwardness of dating, and merge two lives—with conflict, disappointment, baggage, and unmet expectations—is too high? It would seem that for a lot of us, the risk outweighs the reward. Is this why so many of us are single?

I FEEL WRITTEN

For so much of my life, I couldn't approach even the idea of masturbation, let alone talk about it with others, because it carried so much shame. And since shame has an agenda to keep us small, stuck, and hidden, what would happen if we removed it from the conversation? Remember that God wants to be a part of every area of your life.[12] Could it be possible to explore your body in freedom and honor and stay connected to Jesus?

In his letter to the Corinthians, Paul teaches, "'All things are lawful for me,' but not all things are helpful. 'All things are lawful for me,' but I will not be dominated by anything."[13] A few chapters later, he repeats himself, "'I have the right to do anything,' you say—but not everything is beneficial."[14] At this point nuance enters the room.

Should we never drink a sip of alcohol because we may or

may not become an alcoholic, or should we swear off masturbation because it has the potential to trap us in a self-centered cycle? For one person the answer may be a hard no, for another an unequivocal yes. Are either of them wrong? Making this a black-and-white issue definitely makes it easier to teach from the pulpit, especially when we live in a social-media-sound-bite culture. While one-dimensional approaches and sound bites sound good from stage or in a social media post, they disregard that being human is a three-dimensional experience. What if we had space for people to land on different parts of the spectrum?

I also wonder if teaching masturbation as an obvious sin has more to do with who the message is coming from. It seems like every month some evangelical pastor is being exposed for a lack of sexual integrity, from affairs to pornography addiction. Could it be that our pastors' private porn addictions are clouding their perspective? But what if pornography is not your struggle? I wonder if that changes the lens with which we approach masturbation.

In his book *A Million Miles in a Thousand Years*, author Donald Miller writes, "I feel written. My skin feels written. My sexuality was a word spoken by God."[15] If it's true that we are made in the image of God and that God spoke our sexuality into existence, and since pleasure is part of the human experience, then it's possible that the experience of pleasure is a good and God-designed thing. God is for our pleasure, and the existence of taste buds alone shows me that God is for our pleasure. There's just something about the mixture of a good meal and conversation that pushes beyond merely surviving. It nurtures our souls and points us to the Divine. Food wouldn't have to taste good, but it does. It's also worth mentioning that the only function of the female clitoris is pleasure, and God made it that way.

It's as if each layer of what it means to be human ultimately has the opportunity not only to point us to the Divine but also to inspire worship of the Creator. In this sense, an orgasm can be just as worshipful of an experience as a sunset or church service.

This is not a new concept. Most Christians would say that sex not only has the capacity to be a worshipful experience but also can act as a metaphor of the deep, intimate, I'm-not-going-anywhere kind of love between God and humanity. From Genesis 2 through the entire book of Hosea to Song of Songs to Ephesians 5:31–32, Scripture affirms this metaphor again and again. With God, the physical is never just about the physical; it's always an invitation into the spiritual.

If these things are true, then in our commitment to looking at masturbation from all angles and approaching it with curiosity, let me pose this question. While understanding that all God's good gifts can be distorted, if the purpose of pleasure is to point us *toward* God, what might this mean for masturbation?

WHAT IF . . .

For so long I dissociated from my body, judged my sexual desire, and thought both were gross. And because of my conservative background, it has always been easy for me to see how and why masturbation can be toxic and unhealthy. As Lewis implies, masturbation can be a way to avoid and isolate and can be an unhealthy coping mechanism for stress, anxiety, depression, and conflict. We do the same thing with Netflix, food, alcohol, the all-too-familiar social media scroll, and any number of things. However, none of those things are innately bad or sinful. It's the heart and intention with which we approach each that truly matters.

When you feel turned on, instead of judging the sensation, get curious. What are you hoping to accomplish in and through masturbation? What is it you're really looking for in that moment? Are you trying to numb or avoid your feelings? Are you bored, hungry, angry, lonely, or tired? Those feelings are at the beginning of a lot of my breakdowns. Is masturbation keeping you from putting yourself out there and having real-life connections? Are you escaping into fantasyland—to the harem within? Are you addicted to porn? If so, then masturbation might not be for you.

Maybe you've never masturbated or never allowed yourself to explore your body out of fear, believing the lie that your body and pleasure are bad. Or perhaps the idea of touching yourself has felt so gross and sinful, you have felt completely turned off from even going there.

Maybe you want to reassociate with your body after years of judging and shaming it. Or maybe it's just a random Thursday afternoon and you're having a completely normal human experience of feeling aroused.

For me, part of this whole journey has been learning to reassociate with my body and choosing to believe that it and my sexual desire are God-given and good—and in that reality, giving myself the permission to explore pleasure within my body.

So rather than shutting down our desire out of shame, what if we embraced pleasure as a healthy manifestation of being human and in turn expressed gratitude for how God made us? Because, honestly, praise God for designing our bodies to experience so many different forms of pleasure!

ONE SIZE DOES NOT FIT ALL

There's a familiar verse in Mark 12:31, where Jesus says to love your neighbor as yourself. Often we stop at the love your neighbor part, bypassing the rest of the sentence. But this Scripture implicitly teaches that to truly love another, I must first love myself. In other words, the very act of loving myself creates within me the capacity to authentically love someone else. Like the flight attendant who knows I won't be a help to anyone if I don't put my oxygen mask on first, Jesus knows we can't give what we don't have.

This idea may be controversial, but again for the sake of having an honest conversation, let me be blunt: Is it possible that spending time learning to love, accept, explore, and learn our bodies, figuring out what feels good, what does and doesn't work, could help us love, accept, understand, and honor our partner's sexuality in a more holistic way? Because if I judge *my own* sexual desire and genitals as disgusting and sinful, how could I ever accept my partner's?

Now, I ask you: What might loving yourself look like in this season? For some, it might look like rejecting shame around your body, desire, and the idea of masturbation and moving toward a more open exploration that is between you and God. For others, it might look like building stronger boundaries to protect you from self-destructive habits—again, this is between you and God. And for others, it may look like learning to remove shame from masturbation and recognize how God has made your body to experience pleasure. There's no one-size-fits-all answer here, but what I know is this: you are not alone, and God will not leave you hanging in your discernment process.

BETTER THAN CHOCOLATE

In the dedication of his book *The Lion, the Witch and the Wardrobe*, C. S. Lewis wrote to his goddaughter Lucy, "Someday you'll be old enough to start believing fairy tales again." In the New Testament we see Jesus inviting us to become like children once again—to reconnect with our childlike awe and wonder and trust.[16]

When a close friend of mine was a little girl, her aunt caught her masturbating. My friend innocently said, "Oh, Auntie, you have to try this. . . . It's better than chocolate." She's not wrong! When I masturbated as a kid, I wasn't fantasizing, watching porn, or escaping conflict. I simply discovered that when I touched myself in a certain way, it felt awesome. If it's possible as children to explore ourselves in innocence and curiosity, could it also be possible to do so innocently as adults?

Before closing, one thing I want to acknowledge here is this: in the event of sexual abuse, a child's sexuality can be activated prematurely. If this is your story, I'm so sorry that happened to you. It was wrong and unfair, and nothing about it was your fault. When this has been your reality, it can be hard to navigate a conversation around sexuality, desire, and things like masturbation. Know that you're not alone, and be gracious and patient with yourself as you navigate these deep waters.

WHO ARE YOU BECOMING?

In light of all this, do I think masturbation is a sin? My honest answer: yes, no, maybe. I think God is much more concerned about our hearts than behavior modification. I personally think it is absolutely possible to experience personal pleasure and stay 100 percent present in your body without relying on pornography, diving into the harem within, or becoming addicted to yourself.

The first book I had to read when I transferred to Bible school was a little book by John Stott called *Your Mind Matters*. In it he talks about how God created us with rational, problem-solving minds. We should not only use them but use them to the glory of God. He challenges us not to take our pastor's word for it but to seek the heart of God on our own accord, pursue wisdom and discernment, and commit to doing the hard work of asking questions and seeking answers ourselves.

Desire is human; God created it, and He's not embarrassed or ashamed when we get turned on. Rather than judging and shutting down your desire, or using someone else's sound bites as your own, what if you invited God into these spaces, desires, tensions, and questions in order to make an honest, holistic decision for yourself?

Ultimately, our daily rhythms and practices, the big decisions, and the small, in-between, almost forgettable moments of our lives—all point us in a direction. With each breath, we're either moving toward truth, wholeness, hope, redemption, grace, mercy, love . . . ultimately toward God—or not. What are your decisions propelling you toward? One of my pastors, Jon Tyson, asks it this way: "Who are you becoming?"

Is masturbation wrong? I cannot answer that question for you. But I know God desires to speak to us. God is unafraid of your questions and wants to set you free from fear, shame, and isolation. God simply asks you to keep your eyes fixed on Him. He will be with you every step of the way.

TAKE IT FURTHER

1. What has been your relationship with masturbation throughout your life?
2. Between the scientific research on orgasms to C. S. Lewis's "harem within" to Paul's New Testament teaching, what stood out to you most about the different angles of masturbation, and why?
3. Based on the content of this chapter, has your mindset about masturbation shifted at all? If so, how? What questions do you still have?

Chapter Thirteen

LET'S TALK ABOUT SEX

WHAT THE BIBLE REALLY HAS TO SAY ABOUT SEX

Love is a vessel that contains both security
and adventure, and commitment offers
one of the great luxuries of life: time.
Marriage is not the end of romance,
it is the beginning.

—*Esther Perel*

From sex talks with my parents to church sermons to books like *True Love Waits* and *I Kissed Dating Goodbye*, the Christian rule was clear: you don't have sex outside of marriage. Like I said before, that wasn't a huge problem for me because boys weren't necessarily knocking down doors to get to me. Perhaps it was easier to feel prideful about my virginity than deal with the pain of being the perpetual single girl in my group of friends. The validation I felt for staying "pure" kept me going for many years. But slowly, my relationship with Jesus became enmeshed with my virginity.

Most of what I had learned about God and sex was offered by Christian men who got married in their early twenties; it's not that what they said was completely untrue, some of it was, it's just that they had no idea what it is like to navigate dating and sex in today's swipe-right-swipe-left culture. On top of that, they had no idea what it is like to say no to sex for a span of decades as opposed to waiting for a few years post high school.

That bad breakup all those years ago, when my best friend challenged me to figure out what I believed about God and sex, turned into one of the most monumental seasons in my life. Without a broken heart, I don't know that I would've ever had the motivation to embark on this journey.

I started the only place I knew: the Bible. The first thing I did was look up every verse that talks about sex. Turns out God has a lot to say about sex.

AT LAST . . .

We don't even get through chapter one of the first book of the Bible before God starts talking about sex. He creates Adam and says it's not good for man to be alone.[1] But before God creates a partner for Adam, He puts him to work managing Eden and naming all the animals. It's as if Adam needed to see for himself the value of hard work and being a leader, while simultaneously longing for more. Work is important, but it isn't the be all, end all. (Neither is marriage, for that matter).

God puts Adam to sleep, takes a rib from him, and begins designing a separate being: woman. He creates a woman with breasts and curves, and God says all these things are good.[2] Adam awakens to discover Eve. I imagine his jaw dropping to the ground. He is so taken with her that he immediately bursts into poetry: "This at last is bone of my bones and flesh of my flesh."[3] And so begins the first marriage: "Therefore a man shall leave his father and his mother and hold fast to his wife, and they shall become one flesh. And the man and his wife were both naked and were not ashamed."[4]

At a glance these verses may seem small and even insignificant, but they are jam-packed with theological meaning. I'm in my midthirties, and no exaggeration, I've had close to one hundred roommates. In America we move out to go to college, we transition between different cities, jobs, friends, and so on. But in ancient Hebrew culture, moving out meant something; it was a massive rite of passage. And it happened only once.

When a Hebrew man proposed to a Hebrew woman, he went to her home, where she lived with her family. There was no secret dating or late-night "U up?" texts. Her family and friends knew what was up, and so did his. If the proposal was accepted, homeboy had some work to do. The groom would march back to his family home and start to build a house. The wedding wouldn't happen until the home was finished. Often this new home was attached to, on, or near his family property. This was largely because most people had family-run businesses. This means he had a job with responsibilities. He wasn't freeloading off his parents while he pursued his "passion project."

Day in and day out, layer by layer, he built his bride a home. It was a public declaration to anyone who passed by that he was off the market. There was no confusion about where their relationship was headed, none of those confusing moments of *Are we just friends?* or *Is this a date?* or *Are we exclusive?* Nope, there was clarity. This man was a one-woman kind of guy. Through his actions, he showed his bride, both of their families, and everyone in town not only that he was all in but that he was willing to put time and hard work into this relationship. By completing the house, he showed he was a man of his word.

A GENESIS 2 TYPE OF LOVE

Have you ever dated an "I'm gonna" person? It's the person who says they're *gonna* apply for that job, pay you back for that lunch, fix the lamp, save for the house, be on time. But they never follow through. I've been there too many times. The reality is that you marry a person for who they are, not who they say they're *gonna* be. So if you're with someone who constantly says they're *gonna* but doesn't have any follow through . . . you better run.

The Hebrew man wasn't an "I'm gonna" sorta guy. He was a man of integrity, and he did what he said he would do. And not out of obligation. Adam was smitten with Eve. Remember when they met and he cried out to her, "At last," like meeting her was a sigh of relief to his soul; it awoke something in him.

Only after all this do Adam and Eve get married. And then the text says that the two "become one flesh,"[5] aka sexy time. Their souls become one in marriage, and their bodies follow suit. And they hold fast to each other. They're naked and unashamed, and God is in their midst.

What trust and affection these two must have developed in that time of waiting to be wholly naked and unashamed with each other—not only physically but also emotionally and spiritually. Can you imagine it? This is the relationship that kicks off marriage and intimacy and sex in the Bible. It's like God is saying from the beginning, "This is the type of relationship I want for you."

I've been ghosted, stood up, cheated on, bread crumbed, friend zoned, heartbroken, and everything in between. But reading about this Genesis 2 type of love awoke something in me. I want my man to be so taken with me that he's willing to do whatever it takes to fight for me and pursue my heart the way Adam did with Eve. I want a Genesis 2 type of love story.

SEEING IS BELIEVING

Then there's the Song of Songs in the Old Testament. It's like the Bible's guidebook to foreplay and sex. This book unpacks in detail the sexual escapades of King Solomon and his wife.

It's wild to think how hush-hush the church is about what goes on in the bedroom, when the Bible basically has a sexual play-by-play. The book was considered so erotic that some young Hebrew children weren't allowed to read it until they came of age. One Bible commentator said that some Jewish doctors went so far as to advise people not to read the book until they were thirty.[6]

The book starts with the bride declaring how much she wants and desires her man: "Let him kiss me with the kisses of his mouth."[7] She continues by claiming the only place she wants her king to sleep is between her breasts.[8] I love that the book begins with a woman declaring how she wants to be pleased in the bedroom instantly debunking the mindset that says sex is for procreation or that sex is about the woman serving her husband. It's so empowering.

Her affections aren't one sided. The king is equally turned on by her. He declares that her lips taste like honey and his plan is to roll around in bed with her all night long.[9] The bride declares his love tastes better than wine.[10] She offers her consent and invites Solomon to come to her garden and feast.[11] (Yes, she's mostly likely referencing oral sex.) And he does.[12]

The king is captivated by his bride's physical beauty, but it's more than that. He refers to her as his sister.[13] Thank God this doesn't mean he married a sibling; instead it references their deep intimacy that transcends the physical. They are each other's confidants and have become family to one other.

Throughout the book, their community encourages them to be drunk in love.[14] There's no hiding here; everyone knows they're a thing. I dated a guy in my twenties who would never introduce me to his friends or family. What I really want though is a guy who will kiss me at brunch in front of his friends, not just late at night after a few drinks.

Sometimes you have to see a picture of something before you believe it's possible for yourself. Reading Song of Songs showed me a picture of the type of shout-it-from-the-rooftops, we're-all-in sort of relationship that I long for. I want to want my husband the way Solomon's wife wanted him and I want him to want me the way that Solomon longed for his bride. I want to feel confident and empowered in the bedroom so I can say exactly what it is that I want.

All of this has made me wonder why the church has spent so much time shaming people into abstinence and barking out a set of rules instead of sharing about these compelling biblical love stories. I mean forget rom-coms, these are the type of love stories movies should be made about.

SLOW MOVING

Between those sweet honey kisses, the bride says three times not to arouse or awaken love before its time.[15] It's as if she knew I was going to read it and want to grab the next person who crossed my path. So she was like, "Slow your role! And in case you didn't hear me the first time, I'll say it two more times."

God loves sex and spells that out for all to see in this book. But in Song of Songs, we see a precedence of sex within the context of marriage. From my own experience, I know how powerful and intoxicating physical intimacy and romance can be. If it wasn't, I wouldn't have researched every verse in the Bible about it.

I wonder if part of what grounds this explosive relationship between Solomon and his bride is their commitment to each other. Solomon doesn't want a wham bam thank you ma'am. He wants all of her, and she wants all of him. Solomon slowly recounts to his bride all that he loves about her, starting with her mind. He says, "Your eyes are doves behind your veil." The eyes are the window to the soul. Starting here is important because he's saying he isn't only interested in her body; he wants to know her from the inside out. He then goes on to describe her hair, teeth, lips, cheeks, and neck.[16] I don't think a guy has ever commented on my neck. Solomon is in no rush because he's in it for the long haul with her.

Moving slowly takes time. Time allows for intimacy to develop. And intimacy over a span of time reveals commitment. There seems to be something about commitment preceding the physical that creates a foundation of freedom and security in the relationship between Solomon and his bride that I have yet to experience in dating.

HE'S NOT GOING ANYWHERE

God is so taken with humanity, so attentive to us that he knows the hairs on our head and our words before they even leave our lips.[17] God doesn't just know things about us, he knows us intimately.[18] The Hebrew word for this deep sense of knowing is *yada*. There's another time in Scripture when the same word *yada* is used—when Adam and Eve have sex.[19] Author Debra Hirsch offers that "our deepest longings as human beings are to be in relationship with God and our neighbor—this really and simply *is* the human condition. The Hebrew word *yada* ('to know') is, in fact, used for both sexual intercourse as well as our relationship with God."[20] Naked bodies touching becomes a physical expression of those core desires to be fully known, seen, and accepted for all of who we are—imperfections, mistakes, baggage, and cellulite too. Perhaps that's what it means when it says Adam and Eve were naked and unashamed.[21]

Sex has the capacity to offer us tastes of the deep knowing and acceptance of self and another, and it's orgasmic. But it's still just a shadow. Song of Songs depicts the mind-blowing sex of a king and his bride, but just as Hosea's marriage to Gomer in the book of Hosea, it also offers a picture of God's divine love for His bride: the church.

In his book *Theology of the Body for Beginners*, Catholic theologian Christopher West unpacks Pope Benedict XVI's commentary on sexuality: "The Bible has no qualms employing the erotic poetry of the Song of Songs as a description of 'God's relation to man and man's relation to God.' In this way . . . the Song of Songs became not only an expression of the intimacies of marital love, it also became 'an expression of the essence of biblical faith: the man can indeed enter into union with God—his primordial aspiration.'"[22] God desires oneness with us, and something about sex points to that greater reality.

Isn't that the beauty of the longing between lovers—their love isn't motivated by obligation but desire? God is God and has no need of anything or anyone. Yet God wants us. God longs for intimacy with us. As the disciple John so eloquently wrote, the big deal is not that we love God but that He first loved us.[23] God is the great initiator. By God alone are we fully known, seen, and accepted. And He's not going anywhere.

The more I searched the Scriptures, the more I found a multi-faceted, robust, meaning-packed vision for sex, and it was so moving to me.

FORNI-WHAT?

As I moved into the New Testament, I kept finding certain phrases sprinkled throughout: to *flee from sexual immorality and fornification.*[24] I don't know about you, but when I'm at brunch with my girlfriends, we don't typically throw around words like *fornicate.* In fact, fornification is such an outdated word, every time I type it, the red squiggle spellcheck line appears. Even my computer doesn't know what it means.

The Greek word for both sexual immorality and fornication is *porneia.* It's referenced more than 20 times in the New Testament typically in *reference to avoiding it.* It's like the writers got together and were like, "Okay, just in case it didn't land the first time, let's say it twenty-four more times." *Porneia* is where we get the word *pornography*, and throughout Scripture describes everything from premarital and extramarital sex to prostitution to incest, pedophilia and more.

In 1 Corinthians 6:18, Paul tells the church to flee from *porneia*. To flee from something means to run as far as you can as fast as you can, as though your life were in danger—as opposed to getting as close to the thing as you can without technically coming in contact with it. In 1 Corinthians 7:1–2 Paul encourages the Corinth church to get married in order to avoid the temptation of *porneia*. This set of verses is often used during biblical teaching on abstinence.

Daniel Fortenberry, a leading voice on adolescent sexuality, proposes sex to be more of "a pool of experiences." In response, journalist Peggy Orenstein writes in her book *Girls and Sex*, "I'd rather young people think of sex more horizontally . . . as a way to explore intimacy and pleasure, than a misguided vertical race to a goal."[25] It seems at the very least we can say *porneia* includes penetrative sex with someone who isn't your spouse, but based on the varied and layered definitions, Paul perhaps viewed sex as more of a pool of experiences rather than one specific act too. This definitely threw a wrench in my whole everything-but-sex approach. Getting as close to the line as I possibly could was the opposite of the biblical invitation.

BUT WHY?

Years ago, on a whim, I signed up for a half marathon. Let me be clear: I've never been much of a runner. To help motivate me to get my miles in, I joined an early Saturday morning running club at my church. Each week we ran a little farther, and soon each running session was a mileage I had never run before.

As I got deeper into my training, I began restricting my diet. I avoided things like sugar, dairy, and heavy carbs because I noticed that they slowed me down on my long runs. Sugar isn't evil. But my goal of running and completing that half marathon meant something to me, and in the moment, it was more important than a brownie and ice cream—which is saying a lot because I love brownies.

I said no to things I not only enjoyed but really loved, because I had a vision for my future. Abstaining in the moment set me up for success to run and finish my race. Practicing periods of restraint showed me that when I am internally motivated, I actually have it in me to say no to really good things like said brownies for a greater cause. Training for the half-marathon taught me something profound: denial doesn't always equate to legalism.

There's something about practicing delayed gratification that creates a deep resolve within us. Each time we practice restraint in this way, it begins to build a muscle of integrity and inner discipline in us. It shows us that we can follow through with what we say we're going to do. The more we honor our word in small things, the more our character is developed so when it's time for the big moments in life, we're ready.

Saying no to sex isn't about God killing our fun. Perhaps it's more about God using something *very* good to transform our character. When I choose to go to my own bed at midnight when it'd be ten times more convenient and fun to stay in that of some guy, he and I build a deep well of trust in our relationship. Together we are taking a stand for what we value and fighting for something together that's greater than the moment at hand. We are showing each other that even when the going is tough, together, we can take the high road.

International speaker and producer DeVon Franklin and his wife, actress Meagan Good, wrote a book called *The Wait* and share, "Because we waited, we exchanged instant gratification for what we really wanted and who we really wanted to be. Because we waited, God was able to reveal things that we would have missed if we had been blinded by the white-hot light of lust, desperate to fulfill our own desires. Because we waited, we were eventually ready."[26] Later Franklin says, "If you can be disciplined in your sexual life, there's nothing you can't do. The discipline that you create in that area of your life will be the same for the rest of your life."[27] Little else will develop the muscle of integrity, discipline, and character like saying no to sex in the midst of a culture that worships instant gratification.

Perhaps the biblical vision for abstinence is more about our personal growth and transformation than rule-following or proving how pure or good we can be. Even though it's really hard, perhaps saying no to sex outside of marriage is saying yes to a greater invitation. Perhaps an infinite God has more wisdom than my limited life experience. If God invites me to flee from *porneia*, I can know beyond a shadow of a doubt that it is for my good, because God is for my good and He does not hold out on me.

Choosing to delay pleasure and satisfaction, especially when we're saying no to an incredible thing, is countercultural. And isn't that the continual invitation of Jesus? To be a countercultural people?*

WILLING TO WAIT

I'll be honest. I thought for sure after this whole Bible research project of mine, I'd walk away feeling confident about having sex outside of marriage moving forward. But the joke was on me.

---

* Matthew 5–7, The Sermon on the Mount. Echoing throughout the entire Sermon on the Mount as Jesus invites people into a new way is "You've heard it said . . . but I say to you . . ." It's a countercultural battle cry.

With the Old Testament precedent of experiencing sex inside of marriage, and sex being this shadow of oneness, to the repeated encouragement in the New Testament to flee from sexual activity outside of marriage, it turns out the Bible does indeed offer an invitation to withhold from sex outside of marriage. It's frustrating so much of the theology of abstinence gets lost in translation from the historical cultural context to word choice. No wonder it felt so confusing to me.

What I thought would be a few days of googling "sex and the Bible" turned into almost a decade of study, and I have walked away more conservative about my physical boundaries than when I started. But this time, instead of feeling like a victim to Christianity or purity culture, I feel complete freedom.

I have ownership over my sexual desire and feel empowered that the God of the universe cares about me as a whole person and is an advocate for my personal agency. I am shame free, knowing my sexual desire belongs to me. I feel alive and awake to my sexuality in a way that feels both healing and freeing. Because I feel connected to a deeper story woven throughout the pages of Scripture, I actually feel excited about my decision to wait until marriage to have sex.

I want the type of love that's talked about in the Bible. The radical love unpacked in Ephesians 5 and the Genesis 2 type of love filled with passion and pursuit inspire me. And the all-consuming love in Song of Songs is intoxicating. Maybe the New Testament repeats two dozen times to abstain from sex outside of marriage not because God has a low view of sex but an infinitely higher one.

Do I want to have sex? Of course. Will abstinence guarantee me a banging sex life? By no means. I know I have a lot to learn. But the good news is there's no safer place to navigate that than within a safe, committed relationship where you're both all in. You have a lifetime to figure it out.

Will I be really sad if I never get married? 100 percent. Is waiting for marriage to have sex going to be hard? Absolutely. Am I going to make mistakes? Probably. But I've come to realize I want more than just sex. Because when I'm connected to my Creator, the physical is always an invitation to the spiritual. What I want is to experience all the parts within the whole. And as it turns out, I am more than willing to wait for that.

TAKE IT FURTHER

1. Which Bible love story stands out to you most? Adam and Eve or King Solomon and his bride? Why?
2. Why do you think the Bible says to abstain from sex outside of marriage? What are your personal thoughts about sex and pre-marital sex? What questions about sex do you still have?
3. In your opinion, does sex point toward the greater God story? Why, or why not?

Chapter Fourteen

STOP SHOULDING ALL OVER YOURSELF

OWNING YOUR SEXUAL WHY

Timshel—"Thou mayest"—that gives a choice.
It might be the most important word in the
world. That says the way is open. That throws
it right back on a man. For if "Thou mayest"
—it is also true that "Thou mayest not."
—*John Steinbeck*

In one of the most-watched TED Talk videos of all time, author Simon Sinek unpacks how the world's most innovative leaders inspire action. He says most people know what they do, some people know how to do it, but very few people know why they do it. The leaders who connect to the why behind the what are the ones who change the world. After all, Sinek argues, Martin Luther King Jr. didn't say he had a plan; he said he had a dream. And that made all the difference.[1] Sinek is talking about how to lead a successful business, but his wisdom can be applied to almost every area of our lives. Knowing the *why* behind your beliefs and decisions connects you to a greater sense of purpose and vision for your life. Practically speaking, it also allows you to move through the here and now with clarity and resolve.

I can now confidently say I am choosing to abstain from sex until marriage. Notice I said *choosing to* instead of *have to*. Our language is important; we don't *have* to do anything. Shifting my language from *have to* to *choose to* moves me from being a victim to external expectations to being empowered and taking ownership for how I'm showing up in the world. In that case, I choose to trust that an infinite God may know more than I do about intimacy. Because of that, as a follower of Jesus, I am choosing to walk in alignment with the biblical invitation to experience sex inside marriage. Getting to this decision free from shame, fear, and external expectations may have unfolded in a few chapters of this book, but developing my why took a few years. There's no way around it; developing your why takes time.

Part of developing a healthy sexual ethic is giving yourself the time and space to develop your why when it comes to sexual intimacy in your relationships. Knowing what you believe and why about sex and intimacy allows you to determine how you want your physical boundaries to unfold in your dating relationships.

CHOICE VERSUS OBLIGATION

To have a holistic conversation about physical boundaries, the first thing you need to do is give yourself permission to be brutally honest about what you really want, without being judgmental. Saying things like, "I should wait until marriage to have sex," or "I shouldn't go home with him," strips us of the opportunity to connect with what is going on at the heart level. There's a huge difference between saying something like, "I want to have sex right now, but I'm choosing not too because of XYZ," and "I can't have sex because Christians shouldn't have premarital sex." *Should* makes us a victim to external expectations. But when you allow yourself to process what it is that you want and why, you're able to take responsibility for your desire and make a decision from an honest place as to how you want to move forward. Walking into a date with clarity about what your boundaries are and why is unbelievably empowering.

GET REAL

Once you stop shoulding all over yourself, you'll have the space and capacity to process what it is you want and how you want to move forward.

When it comes to relationships, what are you looking for? Maybe you want to just dip your toes in the dating scene. Maybe you're having fun and not concerned about a relationship right now. Or maybe you're looking for a serious relationship that leads to marriage. Whatever it is, spend some time teasing it out. Get specific.

Next, are your actions in alignment with what you truly long for? If not, how can you shift?

What is your ultimate goal for relationships, sex, desire, and physical boundaries, and why?

While you've been reading this book, are there any concepts or passages that have resonated with you? What were they, and how have they challenged your current views? Be specific.

Is there anything you've read that you disagree with? What are those concepts, and what doesn't resonate? Again, be specific.

Up until now, what were your views on sex, desire, sexuality, and physical intimacy? Moving forward, do you feel that anything has changed for you? What are they, and why?

What do you think is the purpose of sex?

Do you plan to abstain from sex until marriage? Why or why not?

My desire isn't to give you a failsafe system but to offer you a trusted biblical framework and vision for sex and intimacy to equip you to seek God on your own accord and make your own decisions. I want you to connect to the core driving force and motivations that propel your behaviors and actions. Are they rooted in fear or freedom? Shame or wholeness? Legalism or your relationship to God?

Legalism says, "It's my way or the highway." And if you make one mistake, you're kicked out of the club. Legalism values rightness over relationship; it says you'll be loved only if you do things right. Legalism requires a constant striving for perfection to earn your seat at the table. All the while, shame taunts you, whispering, "You're such a failure. . . . You don't belong here. . . . Don't let anyone find out how much of a fraud you are. . . . They'll surely reject you, and you'll be all alone." Inevitably, when I don't live up to whatever the standard is, shame comes knocking on my door, whispering for me to hide out in the dark. I've said it before, but it's worth repeating: shame keeps us small, hidden, and stuck.

Legalism and shame are those codependent friends you never liked, but you keep getting sucked into hanging out with them. The only thing they do is keep us trapped in fear and obligation while paralyzing our growth and disconnecting us from genuine relationship with God, ourselves, and others.

When fear is the driving force of our actions and behaviors, our lives become shame-filled, legalistic, and headed toward the dead-end pursuit of perfection. Living this way is as lonely as it is exhausting.

Life with Jesus, on the other hand, is a life filled with adventure, freedom, and wholeness. It's not about perfectionism; it's about relationship. The love of Jesus is free, no striving required.

When we receive God's unconditional love, we have the authority to remove fear, shame, legalism, and perfection from our lives. With Jesus we can trust that all our fumbles and failures are part of what it means to be human. As my friend Ashley says, "Being human is hard."[2] So as we walk more fully in God's love, can we give ourselves and others the permission, space, and grace to navigate this area of our lives?

TUESDAYS ARE FOR SLEEPOVERS

I love how author Sue Edwards approaches relationships. She says, "God does not give us a formula or rule book, although many try to implement one, hoping for a guarantee. He asks us to develop a heart like his. Following a formula is the Pharisee way—not the Jesus way."[3] I won't sit here and say, "He can touch your butt but not your boobs," or "You can have sleepovers but only on Tuesdays," and, "You should wait *this* long before you kiss." Giving you a list of dos and don'ts might make your life easier in the short term, but if I do that, we'll ultimately slide right back into those legalistic shame narratives that propelled so much of the purity movement.

In 1 Corinthians 6:12, Paul tells a group of Christians, "'I have the right to do anything,' you say—but not everything is beneficial. 'I have the right to do anything,' but I will not be mastered by anything." Immediately after this, he talks about how our bodies are temples.[4] Rob Bell says, "This is provocative language. A temple was a holy place, a place where the gods lived, a place where heaven and earth met. The writer specifically uses this image to challenge them with the idea that a human isn't just a collection of urges and needs but is a being who God resides in. He's trying to elevate their thinking . . . to open their eyes to a higher view of what it means to be a human. He's asking them to consider that there's more to life than the next fix."[5]

Right after the 1 Corinthians passage is one of the many times in the New Testament we are told to flee from sexual immorality. Paul thinks this idea is so important, he repeats it again a few chapters later: "'I have the right to do anything,' you say—but not everything is beneficial."[6] In one breath Paul is saying you can do whatever you want while also remaining mindful that your body is a house for the holy.

Hand in hand with this freedom we've been given, we see a warning against comparison in Galatians. Paul writes, "Each one should test their own actions. Then they can take pride in themselves alone, without comparing themselves to someone else, for each one should carry their own load."[7] In other words, Paul is saying, "Folks, stay in your lane! Stop swerving to the left and to the right, and run your own race." Instead of being so concerned with what everyone else is or isn't doing, what if we each stayed in our own lane?

The reality is, there are things I choose not to do in dating because if I did them, I wouldn't be able to uphold my bigger boundary of abstaining from sex. But you may be totally fine with doing them, and that's okay. I have space for that. More importantly, God has space for that. I have a friend who is waiting until engagement for her first kiss. Even though that's not going to be my story, I know her decision was made from a place of freedom. And for that, I honor her boundary. I also have respected leaders in my life who had sleepovers with their boyfriends and were able to remain true to their boundaries.

Having diverse perspectives helps us make holistic decisions. Truth be told, no two couples I've talked to have had the same physical boundaries in dating. There isn't a one-size-fits-all formula. We're dealing with humans, not math problems. But as we navigate our physical relationships, what if we hold in tension both truths Paul offers us: that we have freedom of choice while also being a house for the holy.

One of the most helpful things in determining my own boundaries was having frank, all-cards-on-the-table conversations with people I trusted. The best advice I can give is to do the same: bring all your honest questions, tensions, and specifics into conversation with God and people you trust. I'm confident you'll work your way toward boundaries you can believe in.

TAKE IT FURTHER

1. What are some of your *should* conversations? How are they holding you back from taking responsibility for what you really want?
2. What is your personal conviction about premarital sex? Take time to unpack your *why*.
3. Up until this point, what have your physical boundaries in dating been? What's working and what's not?

Chapter Fifteen

BLURRED LINES

IDENTIFYING YOUR PHYSICAL BOUNDARIES IN DATING

Shame dies when stories are told in safe places.
—*Ann Voskamp*

My sexual past consists mainly of hot and heavy makeouts in cars and at parks and on couches, beds, street corners, and dance floors. There was a smattering of under-the-shirt action here and there, but it was all pretty PG. As my dating life opened up when I moved to New York, so did my sexual experiences. I always assumed staying the night and sharing a bed with a guy who wasn't my husband was sinful even if we didn't have sex. So when I had my first "adult sleepover" in my midtwenties, I was so riddled with guilt that I didn't sleep a wink. I thought if I didn't technically fall asleep, then I didn't technically have a sleepover. If sleepovers were sinful in my book, then being naked with a guy was *definitely* a big no-no. The first time I was naked with a guy, I figured if I kept my panties around my ankle, then I wasn't *technically* naked.

The experience is a montage of blurred vignettes in my mind, but I ended up having oral sex for the first time in my late twenties. The night ended abruptly when I told him I wouldn't have sex with him. He ended things with me the next day. I was devastated that this person, who now knew my body in a more intimate way than anyone else on the planet, in an instant would no longer be part of my life.

Until that night, I never understood when people would say things like, "It just happened." I was shocked at how easy it was to have oral sex and how natural it felt. It was incredible to be that close and connected to another person in such an intimate way, but the breakup was intense. Was part of the reason why because of how far we went physically? Oral sex became another boundary I was unsure of. Was oral sex actually sex?

JESUS + VIRGINITY = SALVATION

I was tied up in a game of technicalities, and the mental gymnastics I played to convince myself that whatever I was doing was okay became exhausting. I spent so much time trying to convince myself I was still a virgin that I didn't stop and realize how much I was idolizing virginity. With my mouth I would've said my identity and worth came from Jesus. But my actions told a story that read more like this: Jesus + virginity + works + the approval of others = salvation.

In church circles I gave veiled answers around what I had done physically in dating, even though in hushed side conversations I found that almost every Christian I knew in their thirties was having sleepovers and oral sex on the regular. A lot of them were sleeping around too, but no one wanted to admit it at small group on Wednesday nights. During this runaround, I still proudly wore the virginity badge of honor since I hadn't technically had sex. The validation and feeling of being better than others that virginity gave me masked how sad I was to be getting older and older with no sign of a partner in sight. I felt half prideful and half insecure and like a sexual amateur.

With my friends who weren't Christians, I'd dread the moment when the conversation would turn and I could no longer hide that I didn't have sex. One time at a party, everyone was going around sharing their sexcapades, and when it came to me, I was like a deer in the headlights. I didn't know what to say, so the words fumbled out of my mouth: "I actually don't have sex. I'm a virgin." It was like a scene from a movie where the DJ screeches the music to a halt and everyone freezes. Those were the longest, most awkward few moments of my life.

Both inside and outside the church, I felt better than, less than, judgmental, ashamed, and insecure all at the same time—and that, my friend, is some bondage.

Peggy Orenstein interviewed young women all over the US for years and found that whether a girl had pledged abstinence until marriage for religious reasons or landed on the complete other side of the spectrum, "they all based their worth, calibrated their self-respect, and judged other girls' characters (tacitly or overtly) based on what was happening, or not happening, between their legs. And they all were still fundamentally defining themselves by their sexuality: by whether, when, where, with whom, and how many times they'd had intercourse."[1] What I've found is that whether you've never been kissed or you've had a million sexual partners or land somewhere between the two extremes, shame tries to attach itself to our stories—shame for not being "pure" enough or for not being promiscuous enough. And since, as Orenstein observed, it's so easy to define ourselves by what we have or haven't done sexually, shame once again becomes our constant, unwanted companion.

When virginity becomes tied to our standing with God, especially for women, this out-of-proportion and unbiblical pressure creates a whirlwind of shame and pride. We chase the lie that our internal restlessness will be satiated only once we get married and are allowed to have all the "legal" sex we want. So instead of pointing people to Jesus, many churches subtly revolve around a more ultimate goal of marriage and the nuclear family. It's no wonder that being single inside the church can feel like you're JV to the varsity married folk. But marriage was never designed to quench our thirsty souls, and a diamond ring isn't the magic antidote to shame. By the way, wasn't Jesus single? If He were alive today, I wonder if we'd judge Him for that.

As much as I actively resented these narratives, they were what I knew for most of my life. Walking away from them was stepping into unknown territory, and it was scary. But if I wanted true freedom, I had to stop worshiping virginity and sexual "purity" above all else.

WHAT IS SEX ANYWAY?

At some point in my life, and I can't pinpoint when or how, I came to believe sex was having a penis inside a vagina. And because of my sexual experiences and my desire to keep my "virgin" status, this definition worked well for me. By the way, young men who pledge abstinence until marriage are four times more likely to have anal sex, and both men and women who make the pledge are six times more likely to have oral sex, all while holding the belief that they are maintaining their virginity.[2]

It wasn't until I started writing this book that I questioned whether I was a virgin. Technically speaking, if sex is defined according to my understanding above, then I am in fact a virgin. But am I?

The biblical vision for sex is a holistic body, mind, soul, and spirit experience. It sounds so epic, but it can also feel elusive. I can't help but wonder if God wanted the whole thing to be a little vague because He knows that as humans we are prone to legalism. Instead of us approaching our relationships systematically, perhaps He longs for us to connect our hearts to His.

A friend of mine got married in her thirties. For years when she was single, she did "everything but sex." It was only after she got married and had sex for the first time that she found she couldn't orgasm through vaginal sex. Her experience is incredibly common. Some studies say that only about one in four women are able to orgasm through vaginal intercourse.[3] One recent study put out by *The Journal of Sex and Marital Therapy* reported that only 18 percent of women reported orgasm through vaginal penetration alone.[4] In other words, around 75 percent of women climax solely from external stimulation. I had no idea.

Also, due to some health issues, sex was really painful for my friend. For all those years, she thought she was saving the "big kahuna" for marriage, when really she was experiencing her personal sexual climax over and over again with many guys. She felt confused . . . had she really waited until marriage to have sex?

This all begs the question: What exactly is sex? And if we choose abstinence, what exactly are we abstaining from? Is it a specific act? When do two become one? When are we no longer virgins? Is sex simply penetration? Is it when we experience orgasm with a partner? Does oral sex count? What about anal? What if a person identifies as LGBTQ+? Can you have sex and lose your virginity only if you're heterosexual? What happens if your partner is impotent? Does that mean you'll never be able to have a fulfilling sex life? I asked close to a thousand Christians to define sex, and almost every single person answered it differently.

GOODBYE, V-CARD

It took me a long time to sit down and look at these questions head-on. I largely avoided them because I was so afraid that with a more nuanced definition of sex, I wouldn't be a virgin.

I also worried I wouldn't be able to uphold my own boundaries if I expanded my definition of sex. But if my identity and worth are truly rooted in Christ, then no matter what does or doesn't happen, I am still a child of God. Whether I'm a virgin or not, God loves and accepts and chooses me. The same goes for you.

When I take into account my own sexual experiences, the definition of *porneia* from the New Testament that encapsulates many forms of sexual activity outside of marriage, and my scientific research on things like orgasm—especially considering how the clitoris is the primary source of orgasm for the female—sex seems way more expansive than one specific act. Categorizing sex as a pool of intimate experiences does ring true to me.[5]

It took me a long time, but I have finally chosen to define sex as any sort of genital penetration. For me this means until marriage I'm choosing to abstain from vaginal, anal, and oral sex. By my own definition of sex, I am no longer a virgin.

CONSENT IS SEXY

With sex clearly defined, we have the clarity to develop a framework to approach our physical boundaries in dating. I want to set myself up for success for the long haul and create a sustainable pace for intimacy within dating.For me, if sex is off the table, then nakedness is off the table. In case you're wondering, even if my panties are around my ankle, I'm still naked. I'm no longer interested in playing mental gymnastics. If I don't want to get naked, that means my pants need to stay on. And if I want my pants to stay on, then below-the-belt action won't be a win for me either. If I want to keep from getting handsy and make sure my clothes stay on, then the whole sleepover thing is a no-go. This means my physical boundaries include basically holding hands, hugging, and kissing. Jesus, help me.

Over the years, I became so used to hitting my hard boundary within the first few dates—sometimes, as you have already read, even on the first night. Back in my "stay out till you make out" days, kissing meant so little to me; it was just something fun to do on a Friday night. Now I want even kissing and hugging to mean something, so I hold off introducing those things for a bit. I want to savor each moment and physical interaction along the way.

Now that I'm clear on what my boundaries are and why, I decide before going into a date what I do or do not want to happen physically. From there I'm able to strengthen my muscle of communication while owning my voice within my dating relationships. Before, I'd get into an unplanned situation with a guy. In the heat of the moment, if it was late at night and guards were already down—and especially if alcohol was involved—it was so much easier to say yes even when outside the situation I likely would've said no. My not making a plan was a subconscious strategy—if something accidentally happened, then I was able to be less responsible for my choices. It would just be an *oops . . . how'd that happen?*

Now before I go on a date, I pause and ask myself questions like: What do I want and not want to happen? Since the communication of boundaries and consent isn't a one-time conversation, how can I convey what my expectations and boundaries are for this particular date? How can I set myself up for success so that I can let my yes be yes and my no be no? One thing I've done to that effect is made a real effort to nix alcohol on the first few dates. As low commitment as it can be to grab drinks with someone, I realized a lot of my physical experiences with guys in New York revolved around alcohol. Alcohol almost always speeds things up physically for me. Moving slowly is already a real challenge, and I want to do what I can do to honor my commitments to myself. On top of that, I want to be clearheaded as I get to know someone.

Setting boundaries, communicating them, and removing obstacles may sound totally unromantic and unsexy. But knowing what we want and being able to communicate that strengthens our resolve and helps us practice healthy consent, therefore actively honoring ourselves and the person we're in a sexual encounter with. And that is a powerful thing.

Let me be clear about a few things: Does not having sex outside of marriage make you a better Christian? No. When the thief on the cross next to Jesus cried out to Him, Jesus responded with profound grace: "Today you will be with me in paradise."[6] He wasn't like, "But wait, what have you been doing in your free time between your legs?" The only thing that makes us pure is Jesus. Salvation is Jesus alone. Grace alone. Does this mean our actions don't matter? By no means. Our actions reflect the posture of our hearts—the beliefs and values we're committed to—but they don't define salvation. Period. The end.

Also, just because I know my why doesn't mean I have it all figured out or that my story will be perfect. I'm a living, breathing human being in her sexual prime, and my body is basically begging me to have babies, like, yesterday. Saying no to experiences I really want to have is difficult. I may blow it at times, and there's grace and space for that. Also, just because I have clearly defined boundaries now doesn't mean they won't change over time. At any point, we have the permission to pause, process, and discern how to move forward physically in our relationships.

Knowing and connecting to God's heart and vision for sex and intimacy does not make abstaining easy, but it does make it easier. The reality is that in every other area of our lives except dating and sex, we're willing to put ourselves out there and make mistakes as we journey our way forward.

The truth is that growth isn't linear, and it doesn't happen when and if we walk through life perfectly. Growth happens in the moments of awareness when we realize we've gone off course and make the conscious decision to course correct.

A GREATER STORY

When my best friend challenged me to do some soul searching after my breakup, I had a lot of desire but no real vision for sex and relationships. Even though I am more conservative than when I started this whole journey, I feel infinitely more grounded and free. Having a biblical sexual framework allows me to be intentional about how I approach dating, singleness, desire, and physical intimacy. I've found that to be intentional is to be awakened to the reality that all our actions move us either toward or away from who we long to become. Hidden beneath the rules and expectations, a far greater question is begging for our attention: Who do you want to be?

We don't accidentally develop character or close relationships. We are intentional about and fight for the things and people we care about most. When we are connected to our why, our hearts have the opportunity to be driven by love and agency. Only then can we make conscious decisions that propel us toward a greater vision that inevitably leads us to a greater story.

It's no wonder dating these days feels filled with so much frustration and disillusionment. We've had nothing compelling us or inviting us into a greater story. But with vision in hand, we can now switch gears. It's time to get to the practical side of navigating singleness and dating in today's swipe-right-swipe-left culture.

TAKE IT FURTHER

1. How do you define sex? Why? How, then, do you define abstinence?
2. Up until now, what have your physical boundaries in dating been? Why? Moving forward, are there any changes you want to make? Why or why not?
3. What are some practical things you can do to set yourself up for success in upholding your boundaries in dating?

Chapter Sixteen

WORK ON YOUR ISH

IF YOU DON'T HEAL YOUR PAST, IT WILL HAUNT YOU

Until you make the unconscious conscious,
it will direct your life and you will call it fate.
—*Carl Jung*

My first true love was tennis. My entire childhood revolved around this one goal: to earn a full athletic scholarship to a Division I college. We didn't have a lot of money, so I couldn't go to the expensive academies, but I did everything in my power to achieve my goal. As a thirteen-year-old, I got the phone number of the number one seeded guy on the high school varsity team and asked to play matches with him. I arrived at the courts early and stayed after everyone left to run sprints and serve baskets of balls. And I did it. I got the full-ride scholarship.

After college I moved cross-country for an internship where I was paid seven dollars a day so I could gain experience in the nonprofit world and work for a company I believed in. After that, I accepted an assistant position with one of the most renowned photographers in the United States. I could barely afford my Southern California rent, but getting to learn from him changed the trajectory of my career and life. After working for him for several years, I made the leap to start my own photography business. I moved from LA to New York City to pursue my dreams of becoming an editorial photographer. That first year in New York, I made less than $20,000 and was so broke I had to share a bed with my friend in a tiny rat-infested Brooklyn apartment. The walls were so thin that my neighbor's alarm clock woke me up every morning. But I didn't care. I was willing to do anything and everything to get my name out there and land my dream clients. And I did.

In college my plan was to get my MRS degree and start popping out babies as soon as I walked across that stage, diploma in hand. But that didn't happen—not even close. Instead of putting my life on hold and obsessing over not getting what I wanted, I walked through the doors in front of me. I allowed curiosity to lead me and took big risks along the way. Each step forward or sideways or backward was crucial and led me to the place I am today. I wouldn't be writing this book if I had gotten what I wanted when I wanted it all those years ago.

Nothing about my career has been linear, but it also hasn't been accidental. Whether making seven dollars a day, or schlepping my boss's camera gear through the streets of New York City, or making $1,000 an hour on a huge editorial set, I've busted my tail and committed to be the best I can be. I resolved that if I didn't get the promotion or bid for the job, it wasn't going to be because I wasn't ready for it or in my own way. I've put in my ten thousand hours and then some. I don't think I'm alone in my experience.

We are an extremely determined culture. We will pay hundreds of thousands of dollars for our education, work long hours in unpaid internships, and move cross-country to climb the corporate ladder and chase our dreams. If we want to lose weight, we put in the work at the gym. Deep down we all know this fundamental truth: how we spend our time and resources reflects our priorities.

Many of us have a deep desire for marriage and partnership. Why, then, does it seem like the thing we are least intentional about? When it comes to dating, Christians seem to be the least intentional people I know. We mask our lack of intentionality with hyperspiritual language, saying things like, "If it's meant to be, God will make it happen," or "I'm just gonna pray about it." I'll be the first to say that prayer is one of the best things we can do. Ever. But just because a door is open doesn't mean you need to walk through it, and just because it's closed doesn't mean you can't open it. And just because there isn't a door anywhere around you doesn't mean you can't create one.

If you want to be a brain surgeon, you're going to have to do more than just pray about it. You have to put in the time, get the grades, apply and be accepted to medical school, do the work, graduate, then apply to, be placed in, and complete your residency. Being proactive isn't playing God; it's wisdom with legs. And the reality is, no matter what, we simply can't mess up God's plan for our lives. We're not that powerful.

Queen Esther's cousin in the Old Testament charged her to get up and fight for her people: "Who knows whether you have not come to the kingdom for such a time as this?"[1] Esther is the only book in the Bible that has no mention of God, but I'd say in confidence that God was at work through Esther's courage and actions. It was Esther's active faith that achieved not only her breakthrough but the breakthrough of millions of people.

YOGA PANTS AND REALITY TV

For years I would sit at home watching reality TV, drinking red wine in my yoga pants with my girlfriends, complaining about how there were no good guys left—they were all already taken. No matter what I did, I always seemed to get stuck in the friend zone. I would download a dating app and scroll for a hot second and then not open it for three months and complain how online dating didn't work—especially if you were serious about your faith, like *me*. Even stuck in a victim mentality, I was still wildly prideful.

My life revolved around female-centric activities from girls' nights to female-led small groups to going to parties and staying in the huddle of girls I arrived with (which, by the way, is very intimidating for any guy to approach). I went to church, work, the gym, and the grocery store with my eyes glued to my phone, scrolling through social media with headphones on. And all the while I wondered why in the world I was still single.

Doing the same thing over and over again while expecting different results is known as the insanity cycle. Being intentional about your dating life doesn't mean you will meet your partner in ten easy steps. Even though I've become incredibly intentional in my dating life, I am still single. However, once we stop having a pity party for ourselves, we can take responsibility for how we're showing up in the world.

If I'm single because that's what God has for me, praise God. I have a good life filled with depth, meaning, adventure, calling, and fierce relationships. But if I'm single because I'm in my own way, then I can do something about that. We aren't passive bystanders in our lives. We are cocreators and collaborators with God. Being intentional doesn't mean you don't trust God with your future; it means you care deeply about the future God has for you. It's time we became just as active and intentional in our dating and singleness as we are in every other area of our lives.

Finally, being intentional in your singleness isn't only about giving online dating a solid chance or talking to the cute guy across the room you've been eyeing all night. Like most things, it starts with a posture of looking inward. If you want to take real responsibility in your season of singleness, the first step is to be willing to look at and heal the trauma of your past.

WHY CAN'T YOU SEE ME?

Over tacos he told me about his failed marriage, his love for God, and how he wasn't ready for a relationship. Instead of red flags, I heard vulnerability. Later that night when we kissed for the first time, my knees went weak. Even though hours before he had told me he wasn't interested in anything serious, based on the night we had, I thought for sure we were headed toward a relationship.

Weeks and months went by, and we continued to see each other sporadically. After each date I thought we must be getting closer and closer to becoming "official," but it never happened. He would slide out of commitment conversations like a magician. Maybe he just needed more time. Surely if he got to know me and could see how great I was, he wouldn't want to lose me. I'd be the one he'd change for. I'd help heal his broken heart. Right?

But he ran around with other women and didn't even try to hide it. Then he'd disappear for weeks on end, but he always kept the door cracked open just enough to keep me hanging on. And that's all I needed to keep barreling ahead.

Even after it became apparent he had no intention of ever taking me or our relationship seriously, I still wasn't done. From sending late-night texts begging him to hang out to stalking him on social media and positioning myself in places I thought he'd be, I desperately chased him.

Like a moth to a flame, I was transfixed.

One night I had a dream I was sitting alone at a dinner table. All it had on it was a plate of saltine crackers with leftover scraps and crumbs strewn about from previous meals. I felt God whispering to me, "Do you trust that I have a feast for you?" I wanted to, but I was starving. I ate the crumbs and crackers as fast as I could. For a minute I felt relief, but the next breath brought with it a hunger and a thirst that were even more intense than before.

I woke up and knew this was about my relationship with that guy. I knew what I really longed for was to be in a committed relationship. But deep down, I didn't truly believe God could have the whole thing for me. So I settled. I inhaled the scraps of attention that guy gave me. Even though it caused so much pain, something felt better than nothing.

It took a long time, but I finally grew tired of the scraps. I poured my heart out to him in a text message. In the moment it felt bold and noble. I was fighting for us! He left me on read and ignored me. A few days later I was on set shooting and got a text from him. It said, "I'm done."

After several years of back-and-forth, our "relationship" was over in a two-word text. I stepped outside between shots, sat on a bench between the New York City skyscrapers, with taxicabs blurring past me, and sobbed. I was crushed.

UNDERNEATH IT ALL

A few short years prior, I was making twelve dollars an hour working for someone else, and now I was the head honcho with a team of assistants. People were running to get *me* coffee. I was making it in the New York City fashion world—one of the most dog-eat-dog industries, for crying out loud. How could I be so bold and confident in my career, but with one look from this guy, all my confidence and self-worth melted into a puddle at my feet? It was humiliating and mystifying. I felt like a stranger to myself.

My "I'm done" moment is what finally led me to find a therapist. We'd sit across from each other in our sessions, she with a notepad and pen, and I perched on the chair desperately wanting to snatch that notepad from her to see if she was writing down what I feared most: that I was a lost cause.

From the get-go she asked about my relationship with my dad. He was the last person I wanted to talk about. We had a wonderful relationship. We talked all the time. Ever since I was a newborn, my dad was the only one who could stop me from crying. My parents called it daddy magic. There was no way I could be just another cliché girl with daddy issues. The thought of it was annoying. I wanted to bark at her, "Why don't you tell me about your daddy issues?" I was incredibly defensive, but she patiently kept digging.

Through my prickly and sharp responses, she uncovered that though my current relationship with my dad was beautiful, for large stretches of my life it was far from it. After my parents split when I was ten, my dad was in and out of our lives, caught in a hurricane of addiction and disfunction. My siblings and I were the collateral damage. Time with him was filled with high highs, low lows, drama, and broken promises. Sometimes we'd search the streets for him at night and find him locked up in some seedy motel. We had intervention after intervention, and he went to rehab after rehab, but nothing stuck longer than a few months. Memories are etched into the walls of my childhood of wading through holidays with bated breath, wondering if he'd show. We lived with my dad in the summers, and he would disappear for days at a time, only to return home shirtless, shoeless, and without a car or dime to his name. He had gone from being a successful businessman to homeless on the streets of Dallas, losing everything and everyone precious to him. Near the end of college, I lost all hope that he would ever be sober on this side of life. Even though he was alive, I mourned his death.

It wasn't a conscious thought, but at some level I believed that if I was enough, he would stop. If his kids were worth it, wouldn't he do whatever it took to become whole again? But nothing was ever enough.

Then something miraculous happened.

My senior year of college, my dad got sober. He started calling me every day to let me know he was sober, in a program, and that he loved me. This went on for months. But I didn't trust him. For over ten years my dad hadn't had any significant periods of sobriety. I begged him to stop calling and told him I didn't want him in my life. I couldn't handle another heartbreak.

But my dad persisted. Looking back, I realize I needed him to pursue me during that time. My wounded heart needed to know that my dad loved me and that he would do whatever it took to restore his relationship to himself and with me. And he did.

Through the years he slowly rebuilt trust, and my heart opened back up to him. What felt like an irreparable situation was repaired. What looked impossible was more than possible. And here's the crazy thing: our relationship was better than before. My dad was present, available, and showed up in our lives any chance he could get. As I walked into a restored relationship with my dad, my heart healed in ways I didn't know possible.

Through counseling, I discovered that who my dad was in my adult life didn't impact me as much as who he was to me as a child. We become attracted to the repeated behaviors, patterns, and relationship dynamics we experience growing up. That's how kids who grow up in cycles of abuse and addiction often become abusers and addicts. What we repeat we strengthen. And if we don't break the patterns, we become and attract the very things we hate. That's how I got caught in a cycle of chasing unhealthy men. It's why I often mistook drama for passion and chemistry. In reality, my behavior with men had little to do with them and everything to do with the young girl inside me, tears streaming down her cheeks, desperately wanting to be enough for her daddy to stick around long enough to get sober.

When you're in the middle of a storm, with waves crashing all around you, all you can do is fight for one more gulp of air. You're just trying to make it through the night. As children we are adaptable, intuitive, and wildly resilient. We learn how to survive. But in Romans, Paul speaks of life with God not as barely surviving but as living a life of abundance: "We are more than conquerors."[2] When you're in constant survival mode and treading water, thriving is impossible. You can't even think about healing and restoration until your feet are on solid ground. I had never fully healed from my childhood trauma because I was too busy surviving it. And by the time my feet made it to dry land, I was ready to move on with my life.

However, when we don't heal our past, it follows us. And mine was haunting me.

SOMETHING ISN'T BETTER THAN NOTHING

Unexpressed trauma becomes trapped in our bodies and experiences. With nowhere to go, that trauma replays on loop, manifesting itself in the relationships and circumstances of our lives until we go back to the wreckage. My hamster wheel of relationships with emotionally unavailable, narcissistic men was proof that I was trapped in trauma. The only way to break the cycle of trauma is to look directly at it, then move through it to the other side. To embark on a journey of wholeness takes a tremendous amount of courage and bravery. It wasn't easy and it wasn't quick, but it was worth it.

Beneath all the trauma, I discovered something else: me. In his book *The Body Keeps the Score*, Dutch psychiatrist Bessel van der Kolk writes, "Beneath the surface of the protective parts of trauma survivors there exists an undamaged essence, a Self that is confident, curious, and calm, a Self that has been sheltered from destruction by the various protectors that have emerged in their efforts to ensure survival. Once those protectors trust that it is safe to separate, the Self will spontaneously emerge, and the parts can be enlisted in the healing process."[3]

In working through the pain of my past, I was able to reconnect with the part of me that believed in love and possibility, the me who trusted that God could have a feast for me and not just scraps. I found that something *isn't* actually better than nothing and that it is possible to break the cycles of dysfunction in ourselves and walk with God into a new reality.

LIKE ATTRACTS LIKE

For a long time I was so mad at men—especially Christian men. Why couldn't they keep their word? Why did they seem so flaky and noncommittal? Why did they only want to be my friend? Weren't they supposed to be better than that? But the reality is, I was attracting emotionally unavailable men because something in me was emotionally unavailable and blocked. Like attracts like, and in all our experiences, we are the common denominator. I don't want to dismiss the pain of experiencing poor treatment from men, but at some point I had to be willing to take a look at how I might be responsible for helping to create and foster those unhealthy patterns and dynamics. After all, it's quite convenient to sit around and blame everyone else for what's going on in our lives.

We can't change, save, or fix anyone. Only God can do that. But we can take responsibility for our part. Our past does not define who we are, nor does it have the power to dictate our present or future unless we let it.

Now, is working on your ish the magic formula for calling in "the one"? Of course not. It's also not the only reason we should wade through the pain and trauma of our past. Whether you get married or not, your wholeness is always worth fighting for. Working on yourself *will* ensure that if and when you do meet your person, your past won't hinder you from your future. If you want a healthy marriage, the best thing you can do is become the healthiest version of yourself.

The first step toward wholeness is to acknowledge your own experiences and to validate them for what they were. Then become curious about the patterns in your life. Once you're aware of the patterns, you can take conscious steps to break free from any unhealthy beliefs, relationships, behaviors, or cycles. Whether therapy, counseling, healing prayer, workshops, retreats, emotional intelligence training, reading, journaling, or a recovery program, the options to pursue your wholeness are endless.

Finally, just because someone may have "had it worse" than you doesn't mean your experience doesn't matter. Pain is pain. And trauma is trauma. Let's stop comparing who had it worse and spend that time and energy seeking healing and wholeness. The truth is, we can't move forward until we go backward, and there is no better time to do the work than now. It will take time, patience, discipline, and courage, and it may cost you money. But you will never regret one penny you spend to invest in your growth and wholeness as a human. Jesus's invitation is to run the race of life and finish strong, not just to limp through it.

I see now that Mr. I'm Done's rejection on that busy New York City afternoon was the biggest gift he could've given me. Experiencing the pain of rejection became the access point to a healing and wholeness journey that has brought me more freedom and growth than I thought possible. For that I will always be grateful for that two-word text. Without it I wouldn't have had the courage to walk away. With it I was able to discover the dysfunctional patterns in my own life that fueled my toxic relationships with men.

Once I looked my trauma in the eye and moved through it to the other side, I was finally able to foster the confidence and self-worth to believe I deserved so much more than the noncommittal leftover scraps of someone's affection.

Here's the truth: change is possible. At every step of the journey, we have permission to rewrite our story. How can you use this season of your life as an opportunity for growth, healing, and wholeness?

TAKE IT FURTHER

1. Are there any patterns or conversations in your life that might be blocking you from healthy relationships? (For example, guys only want to be your friend, or the guy you like never likes you back.)
2. Have you noticed any correlations between past trauma and current sources of pain and heartache? Ask God to give you eyes to see the invisible threads from your past that may be holding you back from your future.
3. What's one thing you wouldn't have learned if you hadn't experienced the pain of a past heartache?

Chapter Seventeen

THE ONE THAT GOT AWAY

THE PRICE WE PAY FOR LOW SELF-WORTH

Just because you know a story by
heart doesn't mean it's true.
—*Ruthie Lindsey*

He was popular, played varsity soccer, and drove a two-door Mustang. And I had a cotton-mouthed, sweaty-palmed, weak-in-the-knees crush on him. Somehow even though he was a senior and I was an awkward underclassman, we became fast friends.

We'd drive through our small Texas town in his Mustang and go to the Dairy Queen for Blizzards. We'd talk on the phone late into the night until my mom would pick up the landline and tell me to go to bed (it was the pre–cell phone era). My parents wouldn't let me go on dates until I was sixteen, so he'd come to my house and we'd sit outside in his car and just talk for hours. Even after he graduated high school, he would drive to come see me play tennis. I was crazy about him.

I eternally felt like the dorky underclassman who had a forbidden crush on the star athlete. I'd think, "How could a guy like that like a girl like me?" The thought never occurred to me that he might like me back.

Eventually, over the years, like most high school friendships, ours faded. Every now and then he'd come to my mind, and I'd wonder what happened to him. But that was about it.

About a decade later, my best friend from high school called me, breathless, saying, "You're never going to believe this." Turns out her boyfriend had lived with my crush postcollege. Apparently, my crush always talked about this one girl. The one that always hovered in the back of his mind. The one he compared everyone else to. The one that got away.

Well, I was his one. Me. He never made a move because he didn't feel good enough for me. He never thought I liked him!

I about fell off my chair.

In an instant, all these moments with him flashed across my memory in a new light. I had never noticed them before because I always assumed he thought of me as a sister. But now when I look back at our friendship, it's hard not to see that he was just as crazy about me as I was him.

Isn't it interesting what does or doesn't happen when we don't believe we're worthy? Because I didn't feel worthy of love, I shut myself down to it. It makes me wonder how many times a guy I liked had been interested in me, but because I didn't feel worthy of him, I was blind to his pursuit.

MINDSET CHANGES EVERYTHING

Paul, one of the great teachers of the New Testament, charged the church of Corinth to be ever so aware of their thought life. Paul doesn't say they *should* take their thoughts captive; he says they *are* a people who take their thoughts captive.[1] The assumption is that they are already a people who understand the power of their thoughts, and regularly examine the source and root of them. He encourages them to keep that up. In Romans, Paul says to allow ourselves to be transformed with renewed minds.[2]

Later, to the church in Philippi, he says, "Whatever is true, whatever is honorable, whatever is just, whatever is pure, whatever is lovely, whatever is commendable, if there is any excellence, if there is anything worthy of praise, *think* about these things."[3] In other words, Paul knew something powerful: our mindsets determine our reality.

We become what we think about. What are you spending your time thinking about?

For most of my life I was stuck in friend-zone purgatory. Repeatedly, I'd like a guy and we'd talk for weeks and months until finally he'd pull me aside to have a conversation. I'd think, "Oh . . . this is it. He's going to confess his undying love for me and we're gonna get married and have babies," only to have him ask if I could set him up with my best friend. It happened enough times that when I liked a guy, I started to expect he'd just want to be my friend. I'd go to parties, spot a cute guy across the room, and assume it'd be another painful friend-zone situation. Why even put myself out there?

Instead of wearing rose-colored glasses, I walked around wearing friend-zone glasses. Everything that did or didn't happen became further ammunition and evidence to prove to myself the narrative I had grown committed to: I was always the friend. So guess what happened for years? I was always just the friend. I thought it, and I became it. My inner thoughts and beliefs shaped the lens with which I viewed and showed up in the world. In being so committed to my narrative, I in turn helped to create that reality.

WHAT WE REPEAT WE STRENGTHEN

A friend of mine keeps an evidence box. In it are quotes, prayers, and random little trinkets, all of them evidence of what God has promised her about her future. People have given her a hard time, accusing her that she's just looking for any excuse to find God in anything. Her reply: of course she looks for God in everything. Why? Because she happens to believe God is on the move to work things together for her good. What if that's true?

What if God is actually working for us, not against us?[4] How would that shift how you showed up in your day-to-day life?

I believe God is always speaking and moving in our lives, but we often miss Him and His blessings because we're not looking for them. Instead, we're on an evidence hunt to prove how unworthy we are, how we'll never find love, or how the breakthrough happens for everyone but us.

I don't think we all wake up in the morning as masochists. These limiting beliefs feel true because we've often had real experiences that act as proof. Our circumstances are real; it's not like they don't happen. Our past impacts our present and can prevent us from our future if we let it. That's why the invitation of faith is so profound. Faith invites us to have the courage to walk into a reality outside the here and now of our emotions and circumstances. It's a more ultimate reality. Faith beckons us to lean into the possibility of the unseen and whispers, "Just because you know a story by heart doesn't mean it's true."[5] Narratives are always on the hunt for new evidence. So if we're going to look for it anyway, we might as well look for evidence of God's goodness and what's possible. To do that, we first have to identify the limiting beliefs we're holding on to, release them, flip the script, and start looking for new evidence.

What narratives are shaping your experience when it comes to dating, singleness, and relationships?

Is it that . . .

all the good guys are already taken?

there aren't enough single men?

online dating doesn't work?
you're always the bridesmaid, never the bride?
you're always the friend, never the lover?
you'll be worthy of love when you lose X number of pounds?
love only leads to pain?

How do these beliefs and experiences cultivate your reality? What circumstances and experiences have led you to believe these are true? How committed have you been, consciously or subconsciously, to proving these narratives? What will it take for you to stop looking for evidence that you are unworthy and that the type of love you long for isn't possible for someone like you? Because what if you're wrong?

What if, even though these narratives feel true, God has something truer for you? Are fear, doubt, and a lack of self-worth at the root of your inner dialogues? If they're not rooted and grounded in love, hope, and possibility, it's time to take those thoughts captive and replace them with truth.

If you want to transform your love life, start rejecting the mindset and beliefs that are keeping you stuck, and go on your own evidence hunt for a more ultimate reality.

Start by noticing the ideas that come up when you think about yourself, dating, and relationships. Simply notice, don't judge. Then make a list. Ask yourself, "Is this rooted in fear or freedom?" Then flip the script. What would be another narrative that would support you instead of the previous one? Finally, look for evidence. The Bible is a great place to start. Speak God's truth over yourself until it sinks in. Look for evidence every single day to support the truth that God is working things for you, not against you. Remember, what we repeat we strengthen. What narratives do you want to strengthen?

The chart on the following pages is an example of my own list:

Limiting Belief	Rooted in Fear or Freedom?	When Did I Start Believing This?	Flip the Script	Evidence
All the good guys are already taken	Fear	After college when most of my friends got married, and I still seemed to be the single one with no prospects in sight. Whenever I ask to be set up, my friends say they can't think of anyone.	It is possible that God could have an incredible partner for me.	God is the God of abundance and more-than-enoughs. Ephesians 3:20–21 (ESV) says, "To him who is *able* to do far more abundantly than *all* that we ask or think . . . to him be glory" (my emphasis).
There aren't enough single men.	Fear	Moving to New York, where single women outnumber single men two to one. The numbers at church are even more lopsided.	It doesn't matter what my circumstances tell me; God is able to bring me an incredible partner.	God is bigger than numbers and statistics. And God is the God who makes a way when there seems to be no way. Isaiah 43:19 (ESV) says, "Behold, I am doing a new thing; now it springs forth, do you not perceive it? I will make a way in the wilderness and rivers in the desert."

(cont.)

Limiting Belief	Rooted in Fear or Freedom?	When Did I Start Believing This?	Flip the Script	Evidence
Online dating doesn't work.	Fear	When I went on the online date with the guy who stood me up.	Online dating has worked for millions of people; it's possible that it could work for me too.	These days, 2.6% of couples meet at church, and 40% of couples meet through online dating.* Online dating isn't going anywhere. People meet online and get married all the time. If it's possible for them, it's possible for me too.
I'm always the bridesmaid, never the bride.	Fear	Probably after I was a bridesmaid for the fifteenth time. It felt like everyone else was moving on with their lives, and I was stuck being the faithful best friend.	Why not me? It is possible that God has marriage for me and that I am not destined to be a bridesmaid forever.	God listens to the cries of our hearts, responds, and is active on our behalf. (1 Samuel 1—the story of Hannah; Luke 18:1–8). Instead of seeing someone else's breakthrough as proof that God has forgotten me or left me behind, use it as evidence of what is possible. If it's possible for her, it's possible for me.
I'm mayor of friend-zone city.	Fear	In high school when the guy I liked went for my best friend.	It's more than possible that the person I'm interested in could be interested in me too.	People fall for each other all the time. Why couldn't it happen for me too?

(cont.)

* Aziz Ansari and Eric Klinenberg, *Modern Romance* (New York: Penguin, 2015), 83.

Limiting Belief	Rooted in Fear or Freedom?	When Did I Start Believing This?	Flip the Script	Evidence
I'll be worthy of love when . . .	Fear	In college when I gained weight, I started to believe I was single because I wasn't thin enough. The girls in my life who were in relationships were smaller sizes than I was.	I am worthy of love as I am today, not some future or past version of myself.	Psalm 139:14 says, "I am fearfully and wonderfully made." Genesis 1:27, 31 says I am made in the image of God and am very good. God doesn't make mistakes. If He says I'm worthy and enough, I am.
Love only leads to pain.	Fear	When my parents got divorced.	Love leads to freedom, wholeness, connection, and breakthrough.	God is love (1 John 4:8). We experience the tiniest fringes of God's presence and love and are forever transformed (Isaiah 6:1). Romans 5:5 says hope doesn't put us to shame. This doesn't mean I won't ever be hurt, but it does mean love is worth the risk.

Now it's your turn.

I know you're probably wondering what happened with Mr. Two-Door Mustang. We ended up reconnecting. When I saw him all those years later, he still made me get dry mouth and sweaty palms; it was like I was an angsty teen all over again. We were both honest about how crazy we were about each other in high school and college. It was such a healing experience. Unfortunately, life doesn't always pan out like it does in romantic comedies. It didn't work out between us, and that's okay. If I hadn't reconnected with him, I never would have understood the cost I was paying for holding on to beliefs rooted in fear.

I made a promise to myself that moving forward I would never again push away love because I didn't think I was worthy of it. And I haven't.

TAKE IT FURTHER

1. What narratives are shaping your experience when it comes to dating, singleness, and relationships?
2. What could be possible for you if you released them?
3. Make a chart like the one in this chapter with five columns: the narrative, fear or freedom, when you started believing this, flip the script, and evidence. When you notice a narrative, add it to the chart and go through the columns.

Chapter Eighteen

DATING IS A CURB, NOT A CLIFF

TAKING THE AWKWARD OUT OF DATING

Not all relationships will lead to marriage.
Some will help you discover new restaurants.
—*Meme advice from the internet (source unknown)*

The only realms where a person *needs* to know if the other person is "the one" on the first date are reality TV and Christian culture. I can't tell you how many times I've walked down the wedding aisle of my mind and imagined what a guy would be like as a dad before we even stepped foot on a first date. And if date number one wasn't totally perfect, and if I didn't feel confident it was heading toward marriage, or if there wasn't that instant spark—without a second thought, I'd walk away. Now, be real with me: Have you ever done this?

As if navigating dating in today's culture weren't hard enough, dating in the church is like constantly being in a fishbowl, with people obnoxiously tapping on your glass. You're trying to play it all cool with your crush, while everyone is snickering and speculating behind your back. By date two everyone wants to know if he's the one. And married people can make this whole dance even more awkward with their incessant questions. For the record, no single person ever wants to answer the question, "Why are you still single?" If I knew, do you think I'd still be single? It's like once you get married you also get amnesia and forget how hard the dating scene can be. Married friends, I love you, and I know you are so excited about us single folk meeting someone. But please, for the love, you need to calm down.

It's no wonder Christian dating is so awkward. The pressure we put on it can be unbearable. Here's the deal: even though navigating Christian dating can feel like a struggle fest, it doesn't have to be. It just takes spending some time to shift our mindset.

ONE STRIKE, YOU'RE OUT

I've gotten so hung up before on trying to figure out if he's the real deal that I'd forget he was a living, breathing person with feelings just like me. God forbid he had an off day or had any sort of nerves. It's like we approach dating by going through a mental checklist and scanning his spiritual résumé, turning it from a date into a job interview. When really, our faith isn't just a box to check but an actual relationship. And relationship with God is like any relationship; it ebbs and flows, has ups and downs, and looks different in different seasons for different people. Just because he doesn't listen to the worship music you listen to, or read the books you read, or follow the pastors you follow on social media, doesn't mean he doesn't love God. It means he's his own person with his own relationship with God. What would it look like if we had space for each other to be on our own spiritual journeys with God instead of sizing up everyone else to fit within our personal brand of Christianity?

Instead of stepping into dating with a one-strike-you're-out mentality, what if we approached it with curiosity? What if we released the grip we have on our agenda and timeline, and simply allowed ourselves to get to know the person in front of us, trusting that over time who he is will be revealed? I wonder sometimes if what we're looking for is more of a spiritual clone than a person who has their own relationship with God.

DROP THE GIRL CODE

Another thing that happens in dating culture is girl code. If after a date or two a guy decides he's not interested, a girl will sometimes blacklist him from all the other girls in her community. Women ask me all the time why Christian guys don't like asking out girls in the churches. This is a huge reason why. Just because a guy goes on dates with multiple women doesn't necessarily mean he is a player. Also, just because you like him or at one time went out with him doesn't mean he's off limits to everyone else. Dating isn't like calling shotgun. We can't stake claims on other people; dating and relationships don't work like that.

REMOVE THE PRESSURE

Sometimes dating feels like we're running full speed ahead over a cliff without a parachute, hoping a knight in shining armor will break our fall. With all that pressure, it's no wonder many guys in the church shy away from asking women out. What if, instead, we approached dating as if we were simply stepping off a small curb? When we release the pressure in dating, we're able to be present and truly get to know someone without there being so much at stake. You can still be intentional with your dating life while letting go of all that pressure.

Sometimes there's instant attraction and chemistry. But that's not everyone's story. I've dated guys and had that initial spark, but when I got to know their heart, I lost all attraction to them. I've also gotten to know guys with whom there was little to no attraction at the beginning. But after I got to know their heart, they became the hottest guy in the room. Attraction can increase and decrease, so give things time to unfold.

It takes time to really get to know another person to see if they're a good fit for you. Have grace for the person in front of you. You don't have to have it all figured out within the first few dates. All you need to know at the end of a date is if you're interested in getting to know the other person a bit more.

TRUST THE PROCESS

One reason I wanted instant clarity on date number one was I didn't want to waste my time getting to know someone if they weren't the one. But getting to know another human is never a waste of time. We're all made in the image of God and have a unique story to tell. There's no harm in giving yourself time to get to know a person. After a breakup when I was nineteen, I told my mom I wasn't going to date again unless he was my husband. It unfortunately took me a long time to realize that to figure out if a guy was my person, I needed to go on dates with him.

If there's some massive deal breaker, like, say, he tells you he's a serial killer, or produces pornos on the side, or is in his forties, jobless, and living with his mom, don't walk out of that date—run. But if not, give it a shot. I practice a three-date rule. If he loves God, he has a job, and there are no glaring red flags, then give it three dates.

Dating and getting to know different types of people helps you find out what your type is. Give things time to breathe, and trust the process.

ONLINE DATING IS HERE TO STAY

If you're not good at dating, welcome to the club. That's what practice is for. No one expects you to be perfect. If you feel awkward with a capital *A*, going on dates will help you get over that. Online dating is a great place to practice things like flirting, getting out there, and interacting with people romantically. The good news about online dating is that people's intentions are known: you're on the app because you're interested in a romantic relationship. There's none of the awkward *Is this a date, or isn't it?* The cards are on the table. Also, you're often interacting with strangers, so if it doesn't work out, the stakes are low. It's not like he's the guy in your friend group you've had a crush on forever, and if it doesn't work out, the whole friend group will suffer. Online is also a great space to practice healthy boundaries and strengthen the muscle of communicating your wants and needs to another person. You can practice telling a guy when you're interested as well as communicating in a respectful way when you're not interested. And many of us need practice! Do you ever start sweating when you just think about telling a guy you like him? Sometimes I still feel like I'm a middle school girl passing a note to the guy I like in class: *Do you like me? Circle yes or no.*

If you want to give online dating a real shot, commit to being active on the app or website for three months. In those three months, aim to go on three dates. That's only one date a month. Go on your app twenty minutes a day for six days a week in that time period. Set a reminder on your phone to open your app for ten minutes in the morning and ten in the evening. Use that time to make your swipes, initiate and respond to conversations, and set up dates. In my experience, you can hardly know if you want to date someone based on an online profile—unless, of course, all their photos are of them taking shots off some girl's belly in a beach bar in Cancun. You just need to be curious enough to meet up. In fact, I wouldn't even consider your first meeting a date. It's just a meetup to decide if you're interested in getting to know the person. If you are interested and have been chatting for a few days, go ahead and let him know you're interested in meeting in person. We're looking for dates, not pen pals, friend.

All in all, roughly 40 percent of couples today meet online as opposed to the 2.6 percent of couples that meet at church.[1] What does this tell me? Online dating can and does work, and it doesn't look like it's going away anytime soon.

TAKE IT FROM RUTH

Remember Ruth and Boaz and how she put herself in the position to be around not just any single guy but one of the best guys in town? Being strategic about putting yourself in spaces and circumstances where you'll be around the type of guy you want to be with isn't desperate or manipulative, and it's not playing God. It's being intentional.

It may be totally out of your comfort zone—and trust me, I get it—but the only way to be open to the possibility of love is to be vulnerable. C. S. Lewis put it like this:

> Love anything and your heart will be wrung and possibly broken. If you want to make sure of keeping it intact you must give it to no one, not even an animal. Wrap it carefully round with hobbies and little luxuries; avoid all entanglements. Lock it up safe in the casket or coffin of your selfishness. But in that casket, safe, dark, motionless, airless, it will change. It will not be broken; it will become unbreakable, impenetrable, irredeemable. To love is to be vulnerable.[2]

My best friend once told me that no one has a bad day when they find out someone has a crush on them. It's flattering. The worst that could happen is that they're not interested in you. In that case, as disappointing as it may be, at least you have the clarity you need to move on. Let's not forget the best-case scenario. They could be totally into you but afraid to make the first move. You'll never know unless you give love a shot.

DROP THE HANKY

I love when a guy brings me flowers or opens the door for me or stands up when I leave the table. As feisty as I am, I'm pretty old-fashioned too. But even in the olden days, we find women making moves. In the Victorian era, when chivalry was alive and thriving, if a woman was interested in a guy, she would look him in the eye, smile, and drop her handkerchief. This would give him the green light. He could then approach her with confidence and clarity.

Men are just as nervous as women when they like someone, and just as scared of rejection as we are. It's funny how we want guys to "man up," when we're not willing to do the same. Maybe it's time for us to woman up. You may wonder why the guy you like doesn't like you back, but he may be totally clueless that he even has a chance with you.

The next time you see someone you think is cute, I dare you to make eye contact for three seconds and smile. You might be surprised what happens. The first time I did this, I felt like I might as well be walking around naked, proposing to guys left and right. But the more I did it, the more I noticed some patterns. I felt comfortable making eye contact with and smiling at guys whom I had zero romantic interest in. The guys I liked, on the other hand, I avoided eye contact with them like the plague. I'd look at the ground or basically anything and everything but their eyes. Until I did this exercise, I didn't realize how afraid of rejection I was and how unworthy I felt of the type of guy I truly wanted to be with. It took time and courage to become more comfortable smiling and looking into the eyes of a man I found attractive. Allowing myself to be seen by the men I wanted to be seen by felt so vulnerable. No wonder the guys I had no interest in pursued me so often—they're the ones I felt safe looking at—while the guys I was into remained oblivious.

You can take it a step further and approach the guy you find interesting and compliment something specific about him or ask him a question. Also, being kind, giving a compliment, or acknowledging something specific about a person isn't being aggressive; it's putting yourself out there in a healthy way. If Ruth could straight-up tell Boaz, a guy she wasn't even dating, that she wanted to marry him, you can go up to a guy and tell him he looks nice today.

I still have moments of insecurity, but the more I practice dropping that hanky, the more I discover that guys are just waiting for permission to come our way. I dare you to try it, and see what you learn about yourself in the process.

KNOW WHAT YOU WANT

Finally, as Maya Angelou so eloquently put it, what if we had the audacity to "ask for what you want" and were "prepared to get it"?

What is it you really want? What are you looking for in a relationship? Maybe you haven't ever been on a date, and you want to be comfortable just talking to guys. Or maybe you're ready to settle down and have kids. Whatever it is, get clear about it. Clarity about what we want gives us a framework with which to move into and through dating.

Know the difference between nonnegotiables and preferences. We often hide behind a laundry list of qualities in a partner that quite frankly are unattainable by a mere mortal.

He has to be taller than we are, handsome with a six-pack, have a solid 401(k), and, oh yeah, love Jesus too—in other words, a Brad Pitt version of Jesus. My nonnegotiables are primarily character based. I want a man who loves Jesus and loves people really well and has integrity, character, and a vision for his life. I'm looking for someone who sees me and is unintimidated by my strength. I'm also looking for someone I can laugh with, because life is hard, and the day-to-day is mundane and not sexy. So we'd better at least be able to laugh about it. Obviously physical attraction and sexual attraction are nonnegotiables because, at the end of the day, if you don't want to have sex with them, they're just a friend, not a partner. Another thing that's important to me is that he has a job. That doesn't mean he needs to be a millionaire flying around on private jets, and I understand the pain of unexpected job loss and when things are truly out of your hands in circumstances, say for instance like a global pandemic. But generally speaking, having a job or actively pursuing work reveals a sense of work ethic, responsibility, and financial stability.

Now, my preferences would be things like his being tall, dark, and handsome and a former professional athlete. Or I would love the option to be able to stay at home when I have kids. What's great about knowing your nonnegotiables and preferences is it allows you then to turn them back on yourself.

A few years ago, when I was neck deep in debt and could hardly pay my rent, I was praying for a husband who was financially secure. I realized I was looking for a sugar daddy and financial savior as opposed to a partner. It was convicting. If I want a financially stable spouse, I get to be that first. I'm happy to say I'm finally debt free. Thank you, God!

Are you holding yourself to the same standards you're holding your future spouse to? If not, what do you need to work on?

Remember to keep the main thing the main thing. In other

words, keep your preferences where they belong—as preferences. I can't tell you how many women I know who had no initial attraction to their partners but who are now head over heels in love with and attracted to them. Love often looks a lot different than how we think it will. Be open to the unexpected, and allow yourself to be pleasantly surprised.

The balance is learning how to have a real sense of clarity while also making sure you don't have a death grip on your "list." So get clear. Ask God specifically for what you want, and then surrender it. Trust that God loves giving good gifts to you. Our faith is built with every answered prayer. I don't know about you, but I want to see God move in my love life. So I'm going to keep asking God to bring love into my life. And I'm going to take God's Word to heart and believe that hope won't put me to shame.[3] If you're bold, try thanking God in advance for what He's yet to do. Be expectant, and see how your faith may expand exponentially. Isaiah 43:19 says, "See, I am doing a new thing! Now it springs up; do you not perceive it? I am making a way in the wilderness and streams in the wasteland." This is the battle cry over my marriage and my future.

Don't lose heart, hold fast to hope, and keep choosing to be vulnerable with your heart. Even if, like me, you've prayed to God a million times and you feel like He's answering every prayer but this one—God hasn't forgotten you. He hears you. He has good things for you. He loves doing impossible things, and He loves making a way when there doesn't seem to be a way. It's what He does; it's who He is.

TAKE IT FURTHER

1. Are there any ways you have been part of the problem, like me, in making dating more awkward than it has to be? How so, and what can you do instead to reduce the pressure?
2. This week, make eye contact and smile for three seconds with at least one person you find attractive.
3. What are your top three nonnegotiables in a partner and your top three preferences, and why?

Chapter Nineteen

NOW WHAT?

She is sensitive enough to the wind to know
when she needs to start walking away,
and she doesn't mind how long the journey will take
because even on days she can't shake the fog,
she trusts she has never really been in control.
And she has seen a succulent survive enough times to know
she is much stronger than she thinks.
—*Danielle Bennett Simmons*

Ever since I was a little girl, I've wanted to be a wife and mama. Maybe it's because I had a stay-at-home mom or because I'm one of six kids and loved the bustle of growing up in a house full of people. Maybe it's because historically that's what has been expected of me. Or perhaps because that's what many Christian women aspire to be. Or maybe it's purely because, ever since I was a little girl, I've wanted to be a wife and mama. (By the way, if you're a woman and you don't desire marriage or children, you're not less of a woman.)

Because of that desire, for so long my life has revolved around doing whatever I can to position myself to meet my person. I've gone to parties I didn't want to go to because chances are, I'm not going to meet someone when I'm watching rom coms at home in my sweatpants. I've dated guys I didn't want to date because I feared my standards were too high. And maybe, just maybe, if I gave it a chance, things would magically work out. I've settled for crappy treatment from mediocre men because something felt better than nothing. I've done crazy, embarrassing, and desperate things in hopes of proving myself to men who weren't interested in me.

And for years I felt like God was holding out on me, like everyone else was getting a membership to some club, and my application kept getting lost in the mail. I was living, but not fully. It felt like my life was on pause, and it would start once I met my person.

If my life unfolded the way I thought it would, I would've graduated college with my Bible degree and a diamond engagement ring on my finger. By now my life would be filled with kids gearing up for their SATs and driver's permits. But here I am typing this final chapter, single as ever. And you know what? Thank God. If I got what I wanted when I wanted it, I never would have moved to California. I never would have traveled the country living out of a van with two other people, doing advocacy work for a cause I deeply believed in. I wouldn't have worked for that photographer who opened up a whole other world to me. I probably wouldn't have skinny-dipped in Guatemala, bungee jumped into the Nile River, backpacked through Italy, drunk red wine under the Eiffel Tower at midnight, snuck into New York Fashion Week, or danced in the pouring rain in the middle of Brooklyn Bridge at two o'clock in the morning. I wouldn't have met the people over the years who have challenged who I am as a human, as a woman, as a believer. I wouldn't have had the gift of being dumped, rejected, and ghosted as many times as I have been. Without the heartbreak, my blind spots wouldn't have been revealed. I wouldn't have experienced the growth and healing that each tear has brought forth. I definitely wouldn't be writing this book, and I 100 percent wouldn't be the woman I am today.

It's not that my plans were bad or small; it's just that God's plans for our lives are more creative than we could ever imagine.[1] I think about Hannah in the Old Testament all the time. The biggest breakthrough she could imagine was to be able to have one child. For a barren woman, that alone would've been miraculous. But God had other plans. She ended up with not one but six children. Sometimes I wonder if God is waiting for us to surrender the dreams that feel so precious to us so He can roll out the miraculous. Ephesians 3:20 says, "To him who is able to do immeasurably more than all we ask or imagine . . ." What if we really believed that? If God's plans are far greater than anything we could ever imagine, then why not dream far and dream wide? What if we released the death grip we have on how we think life is supposed to turn out, trusting that our biggest dreams might be only scratching the surface of what God has for us. Why not pursue your purpose as if your life depended on it, because maybe it does? Have the audacity to have an epic vision for your life, run wildly after your dreams, and hold the tension of both your plans and God's with open hands.

DIAMOND RINGS DON'T GIVE YOU PURPOSE

Jesus lived a provocative, scandalous, adventurous life. He had deep and intimate relationships with both single and married men and women. He was friends with young children and the elderly. Those ostracized from culture felt safe, seen, and known by Him. The ones who felt judged and condemned by the religious were met with kindness, acceptance, and love from Jesus. He was friends with people who didn't believe what He believed about God or life, and He loved them purely, without an agenda. Jesus modeled a life of radical community, and it was so compelling that thousands of years later, the ripple effects of His holistic love for people pulse throughout this world. He was single and seemed to live a pretty epic life without a partner. Jesus was uninhibited by His relationship status.

The truth is, your life isn't on hold until you meet the one. Diamond rings don't give you purpose, and you're not less than because of your relationship status. You have purpose pulsing through your body, and there are stories, gifts, and talents inside you that are aching to come out. What's that thing inside you that's begging to come out? What's that thing that when you talk about it, your eyes light up, your heart beats a little faster, and your hand gestures become bigger and bigger? Do more of that thing. You may not have just one thing but a thousand little things over the span of your life that will morph and take shape over time. Author Jen Hatmaker cries, "The world is hungry for women who show up and tell the truth, unafraid and free, expanding to the very edges of who they were always meant to be."[2] God is the master storyteller, and He created you with a story to tell. It's in your bones, and it's begging to speak to the world.

If you want to be who you were always meant to be, start by getting to know yourself. Figure out what you believe about God, yourself, others, life, love, sex, desire, and all the things. Step into those in-between spaces; have the courage to step into the gray. Allow yourself to be led with a posture of curiosity. Give yourself the permission to doubt and ask questions until you're blue in the face, and then ask more. Why do you believe the things you believe? Who is God? Who is God not? Let Scripture surprise you. Don't take your pastor's word for it, and definitely don't take mine. Be willing to do your own work, research, seeking. Through it all, never underestimate the power of prayer. I don't understand how it works, but I've experienced it in my own life and read it a hundred times over in the Bible: the heart of God is moved to compassion when He hears the cries of His people. God is not some harsh judge waiting in the shadows for you to blow it, but a tender lover eager to be intimately connected with you.[3]

If you're single because that's the life God has for you, praise God. He's not holding back on you. If you're single because you're in your own way, then work on your ish. Take responsibility and ownership for how you are showing up in your life. Get to know yourself, and I mean really get to know yourself. Why do you do the things you do? Is your past haunting you and keeping you from your future? Go to therapy. Get support. What lies and narratives are keeping you stuck in shame? Fight for your wholeness the way you'd fight for your best friend's. Identify the fears, limiting beliefs, lies, and hang-ups that prevent you from your future and block your growth. Rip them out by their roots, and replace them with truth, love, hope, compassion, and grace. Your pain will become your greatest message and testimony to a world that longs to know they are not alone.

God created you for an abundant life. Be the person who has the courage to do the work. Pursue wholeness because you're worth it. Do it because just as hurt people hurt people, free people free people, and what we repeat we strengthen. What do you want to strengthen? What would open up for you if you were able to walk through your life in freedom? What injustices do you see in the world around you, and how can you actively be a part of moving the needle forward toward healing, restoration, and redemption? Have the guts to step outside the box. You might ruffle some feathers, you may be misunderstood, but oh well. You're in good company—I came out of the womb ruffling feathers.

Think bigger, dream harder, and then get to it. Author Shauna Niequist's words speak the language of my soul:

> I have always, essentially, been waiting. Waiting to become something else, waiting to be that person I always thought I was on the verge of becoming, waiting for that life I thought I would have. In my head, I was always one step away. In high school, I was biding my time until I could become the college version of myself, the one my mind could see so clearly. In college, the post-college "adult" person was always looming in front of me, smarter, stronger, more organized. Then the married person, then the person I'd become when we have kids . . . And through all that waiting, here I am. My life is passing, day by day, and I am waiting for it to start. I am waiting for that time, that person, that event when my life will finally begin.[4]

Your life is here. The grand moment you're looking for is right now. Don't let it pass you by as you wait for your life to start. And guess what? It's going to be messy. You're going to get hurt, fumble your way forward, and take detours along the way. It's not going to turn out how you planned, and only in hindsight will you be grateful it didn't. You're going to do and say things you wish you hadn't. You're going to blow it a thousand times a day, and it'll all be worth it. Because growth isn't the moment when we attain perfection but the moment we realize we've gone off course and make the conscious decision to get back on track. (Plus, people who spend their lives trying to be perfect are no fun to be around.)

It matters to the world that you step fully into who you are. If you're waiting for permission to start living, here it is: you have permission. The big secret is that you've had it all along.

I KNOW THAT I KNOW THAT I KNOW

For years now I've plowed through research data, graphs, charts, books, articles, commentaries, and sermons, and I've painstakingly combed through and scoured the Bible looking for answers to my biggest questions about sex, sexuality, and desire. I've processed and prayed with my fists shaking toward the sky, begging for clarity—all in hopes of unearthing a biblical vision for singleness, sex, desire, and intimacy that far surpasses the cheap, shame-filled sexual scripts and list of dos and don'ts that so many of us were given. Never in a million years would I have guessed the richness of the God-story surrounding sex that I found sprinkled throughout the pages of Scripture.

I never could have anticipated how life-changing the journey of asking the hard questions about sex and God would have ended up being for me. Only when I stepped into the shaky unknown was I able to quiet all the clanging noises and voices barking at me about who I am and what is true. It was in that place I began to encounter a God who is much bigger, kinder, more loving, and more expansive than the one I tried to contain in a nice and neat black-and-white box for most of my life. And it was in the process of getting curious about who I am outside of who I have been told to be that I met another pretty incredible person: me.

It was in the deconstruction that I began to discover something new: My own voice. My own desires. My own beliefs. My own relationship with God. Moving through the questions and the doubt, seeking God on my own accord, searching the Scriptures finally allowed me to discover and reconstruct a healthy and biblical sexual ethic that honors my values and the God-image in me and gave me what I needed to walk out this season of singleness with freedom and clarity. It was scary at times, and really hard, but it was so worth it. I know it will be for you too.

I've spent all this time working through my past, reclaiming my worth and identity, stepping into my calling, and becoming the person I was always meant to become. What if, after all this, I still end up all alone? What if I become the crazy cat lady, watching *Friends* reruns all by herself and talking to a wall? I'll be real with you: that'd be devastating.

But if there's anything I've learned in my thirty-some years of being a single woman, having been a bridesmaid seventeen times, and having photographed weddings full-time for over a decade, it's this: marriage isn't the answer. It won't fulfill you, and it's not the antidote to all your problems. Neither is sex, for that matter. I finally know that I know that I know that I'd rather be single than be with someone who isn't God's best for me. I finally trust that my life isn't on pause until a diamond ring sparkles on my finger. Do I still want to get married? Do I still really want to have sex? Yes. Absolutely. I'll keep hoping, praying, and believing for it because God is able to do it. But regardless of whether I ever get the things in life I want or long for, God is good. God is better than any person, thing, or gift we could ever desire. The ultimate goal is Jesus, not the things He does or doesn't give us.

Your purpose is not defined by your relationship status. Your character is not developed through instant gratification. Your identity is not rooted in your sexual desire. Your sexuality doesn't exist solely within the confines of marriage, nor only for your spouse. Your salvation doesn't hinge upon your virginity. You are *imago Dei*, made in the image of God—that's who you are. Your sexuality belongs to you, and regardless of what you have or haven't done, you get to have a seat at the table. You are whole today, not someday when. Why? Because God says so. Period. The end.

We've covered a lot of ground, and I've expected a lot from you. I've asked you to take a mirror and look directly at yourself and your theology. I've urged you to confront the why behind your beliefs and views on sexuality, desire, identity, and intimacy. I didn't do it to make you wrong or because I hate culture or the church. Quite the opposite. It's my love for the church that propels me to speak with such boldness. The purity movement did not work. And the one-dimensional sexual narratives we took from it have cast shame and disillusionment on millions of people. Church, we must do and be better.

If you walk away with a script to regurgitate to your boyfriend about why you won't have sex before marriage or why he can or can't touch your boobs, I've failed you. My hope is that you are equipped to dig deeper into your own story. And as you do, I hope you discover a God with greater vision and a deeper love for you than you ever could have imagined. I may have left you with more questions than answers. I wish I could say I was sorry about that, but I'm not. This is life, not the movies. And life doesn't end with beautifully wrapped boxes with perfect little bows on them.

My story is still being written, and so is yours. What I can leave you with is this: a battle cry to discover your own voice, to get to know the tender voice of God, and to live a radical, intentional, shame-free, freedom- and hope-filled, creative, purposeful, and unapologetic life. Life is happening all around us, unfolding before our very eyes, beckoning us to come play. What do you say we dive in?

With you on the journey,

TAKE IT FURTHER

1. What are three things you are taking away from our time together?
2. What questions do you still have?
3. What might it look like to step fully into "doing the work" and pursuing your purpose?

ACKNOWLEDGMENTS

This morning I'm writing from a Brooklyn hotel room, tucked under a white comforter that probably hasn't been washed in ages and wearing the hotel robe. I've locked myself in this room until I'm done with this book, and I'm tired. Like, soul tired. My eyeballs hurt from staring at my computer screen, and my brain feels like mush.

I don't know if I've ever done anything as stretching and scary as writing this book; it has felt just about as vulnerable as walking down a busy Manhattan street butt naked, making direct eye contact with everyone I pass by. I honestly didn't think I could do it. I'm the girl who almost failed a remedial writing class her last semester of college. I've never considered myself a writer, or a good one at that. Nothing about this process has been light or easy, and truth be told, if it weren't for the wild and committed people that I love dearly and do life with, I would've thrown in the towel and walked away long ago. As I sit here, locked away in this hotel room, I'm filled with and fueled by prayer and encouragement, standing on the shoulders of people who believe in me continuously even though I doubt myself constantly. I am overwhelmed with gratitude.

To my editors, Stephanie and Kim—your support, feedback, and notes have taken my ragtag story and shaped it into a book I am incredibly proud of. Thank you for stretching me beyond what I thought I was capable of. And to the team at Zondervan and HarperCollins—you have put up with my endless opinions, questions, and pushback with grace and given me the space to share my story as it really unfolded. "Thank you" hardly describes the feeling I have for you.

Jamie Ivey, your having me on your podcast all those years ago ended up being a huge catalyst for me to meet my agent Jana, whom I "accidentally" sat next to at your conference in Texas. Jana, you have relentlessly believed in me, fought for me, and responded to my self-indulgent, pity-party, I-can't-do-this-I'm-not-the-girl-for-the-job texts and voice memos. This entire process has felt like someone threw me in an ocean and told me to breathe under water. And you have shown me that I've been able to do just that all along. Thank you.

To Ashley Abercrombie and Boronia—my book wouldn't exist without the hours upon hours you took out of your days to read and reread these chapters. You shone many a light on my blind spots, and your insight has been priceless. Thank you.

Elizabeth, you walked with me hand in hand through my exploration of doubt and self-discovery surrounding sex and sexuality, and you had space for me to be on the journey. Along with Marina, Jen W., Rachel, Angela, Lindsey B., Francesca, and Amanda, you offered love and support as opposed to judgment and condemnation. I didn't know it at the time, but that was exactly what I needed. (I'm confident I've forgotten women who deserve to be on this page—please forgive me. I love and adore you.)

Sara, you lived my heartache with me in real time and encouraged me all those years ago to figure out what I believed about sex. You are a true friend and soul sister. I love you forever and am so glad you created a perfect little human: Levi. Levi, I know you're just a baby, but someday you might think it's cool that your name is in a real-life book.

I can't leave out all the guys who have broken my heart, left me in the lurch, and dumped me. I don't regret any of it. I'm grateful not only for you but for what I learned through your rejection. Thank you for walking away when I didn't have the courage to do so myself.

To Mom; Dad; Danny; Paul; Caroline; Laura Lee; Lilly; Grace; Aunt Ann and Uncle Barry; Andi Andrew; David Kim; Kitty; Mary, Steve, and Josh Farrar; Kait Warman; Tiffany Bluhm; Kelsey Chapman; and the dozens of other people who have called me, written me letters, sat down with me over coffee, made dinners for me, sent me texts at the exact moment I needed them, brainstormed book ideas with me, cried with me, prayed with me, and believed with me—I have a lifetime of gratitude for you.

It almost feels trite to thank God—like I'm some musician accepting a Grammy. But trite or not . . . God, thank you for being real, for endlessly pursuing my heart, for being the ultimate source of grounding peace, love, safety, and security, and for pointing me to a hope that constantly surpasses any of my expectations—I love you. My life is yours.

And finally, to you, for taking the time to read this book and journey with me through the Chutes and Ladders game that is my story. Wow. Thank you.

NOTES

Introduction

1. See Peggy Orenstein, *Girls and Sex: Navigating the Complicated New Landscape* (New York: HarperCollins, 2017), 93.
2. My friend Jedidiah Jenkins taught me the phrase "sexual infant," and I don't know if I've ever felt so known. Jedidiah Jenkins, *To Shake the Sleeping Self: A Journey from Oregon to Patagonia, and a Quest for a Life with No Regret* (New York: Convergent, 2018), 103.
3. "Eastern Philosophy—Kintsugi," The School of Life, February 12, 2016, YouTube video, 3:58, https://www.youtube.com/watch?v=EBUTQkaSSTY.

Chapter 1: My Breaking Point

1. *Elf*, directed by Jon Favreau, written by David Berenbaum (New Line Cinema, 2003).
2. Wendy Shalit, *A Return to Modesty: Discovering the Lost Virtue* (New York: Free Press, 1999). This book is all about how the free sex movement didn't liberate women but created more bondage. She argues one of the most feminist moves we can make is to return to modesty.
3. Matthew 7:24–27.
4. Psalm 127:1.
5. Proverbs 16:21.

Chapter 2: Modest Is Hottest

1. Chimamanda quotes something similar in her book: "We teach **girls** that they cannot be **sexual beings** in the way that boys are." Chimamanda Ngozi Adichie, *We Should All Be Feminists* (New York: Anchor, 2014), 32.
2. Adichie, *We Should All Be Feminists*, 33.
3. Peggy Orenstein, *Girls and Sex: Navigating the Complicated New Landscape* (New York: HarperCollins, 2017), 11.
4. Genesis 1:26–31.
5. Genesis 1:26–31.
6. Orenstein, *Girls and Sex*, 12.
7. "Yeah!" featuring Lil' Jon, Ludacris, track 2 of Usher, *Confessions* (Arista, 2004).
8. Ariel Levy, *Female Chauvinist Pigs: Women and the Rise of Raunch Culture* (New York: Free Press, 2006), 31.
9. Peggy Orenstein, *Girls and Sex: Navigating the Complicated New Landscape* (New York: Harper Collins, 2016), 14.
10. Adichie, *We Should All Be Feminists*, 39.
11. Adichie, *We Should All Be Feminists*, 38–39.
12. Wendy Shalit, *A Return to Modesty*: *Discovering the Lost Virtue* (New York: Free Press, 1999), xxii, xxv.
13. 1 Corinthians 13:7–8.
14. Shalit, *A Return to Modesty*, 78.

Chapter 4: The Time I Became a Feminist

1. Genesis 1:26–31.
2. Ruth 3:1–18.
3. Ruth 4:15 ESV.
4. 1 Samuel 13:14.
5. 1 Samuel 1:6–7.
6. 1 Samuel 1:5, 8.
7. 1 Samuel 1:1–2:21.
8. Proverbs 31:15.
9. Proverbs 31:16.
10. Proverbs 31:18.
11. Proverbs 31:26, 28–29.
12. Proverbs 31:26, 31.
13. Matthew 1:18–21.

14. John 4:1–42.
15. John 8:1–11.
16. Luke 7:36–50.
17. Luke 7:44.
18. Luke 7:44–47 ESV.
19. Carrie A. Miles, *The Redemption of Love: Rescuing Marriage and Sexuality from the Economics of a Fallen World* (Grand Rapids: Brazos, 2006), 65.
20. Luke 8:1–3.
21. Acts 16:14–15.
22. Romans 16:1–2.
23. Dan Brennan, *Sacred Unions, Sacred Passions: Engaging the Mystery of Friendship between Men and Women* (Elgin, IL: Faith Dance, 2010), 119–20.
24. Brennan, *Sacred Unions, Sacred Passions*, 123.
25. 1 Timothy 2:12.
26. Esther 4:14.
27. Dictionary.com, s.v. "Feminist," accessed September 18, 2020, https://www.dictionary.com/browse/feminist?s=t.

Chapter 5: Submit to My Husband . . . What Does That Even Mean?

1. Ephesians 3:9–13.
2. Ephesians 2:12.
3. Ephesians 5:1–21.
4. Mark 11:15–18.
5. John 13:1–17.
6. Luke 7:1–10.
7. John 14:26.
8. Matthew 28:20.
9. Ephesians 3:15–19.
10. Matthew 7:21–23.

Chapter 6: Stay Out Till You Make Out

1. Rob Bell, *Sex God: Exploring the Endless Connections between Sexuality and Spirituality* (Grand Rapids: Zondervan, 2007), 53.
2. Bell, *Sex God*, 52.

3. Kiersten White, *The Chaos of Stars* (New York: HarperCollins, 2013), 258.
4. If you want to lean more into this idea, read chapter 2, "God Wears Lipstick," in Rob Bell's book *Sex God*.

Chapter 7: A Real-Life Prude Unicorn

1. Dr. Celeste Holbrook, "Our Story," accessed September 18, 2020, https://www.drcelesteholbrook.com/our-story.
2. *Mean Girls*, directed by Mark Waters, written by Tina Fey (Paramount Pictures, 2004).

Chapter 8: Stepping into the Gray

1. Matthew 21:12–13.
2. Luke 19:1–10.
3. John 8:1–11.
4. John 8:7.
5. John 8:10.
6. John 8:11 NLT.
7. Matthew 5–7.
8. This definition came from Dr. Ron Proctor, my spiritual formations professor at Dallas Baptist University. Sitting under his teaching for two semesters transformed my life.
9. Genesis 1:26 NLT.

Chapter 9: Two Sides of the Same Coin

1. Genesis 1:31 CEV, emphasis mine.
2. Matt Chandler, *The Mingling of Souls: God's Design for Love, Marriage, Sex, and Redemption* (Colorado Springs: Cook, 2015), 13.
3. Chandler, *The Mingling of Souls*, 13.
4. Bruce Marshall, *The World, the Flesh, and Father Smith* (Boston: Houghton Mifflin, 1945), 108.
5. James H. Olthuis, "Be(com)ing: Humankind as Gift and Call," *Philosophia Reformata* 58, no. 2 (December 17, 1993): 153–72, https://doi.org/10.1163/22116117-90000062.
6. Debra Hirsch, *Redeeming Sex: Naked Conversations about Sexuality and Spirituality* (Downers Grove, IL: InterVarsity Press, 2015), 26.

7. Marva Dawn, *Sexual Character: Beyond Technique to Intimacy* (Grand Rapids: Eerdmans, 1993).
8. Hirsch, *Redeeming Sex*, 66–67.
9. Psalm 42:1, emphasis mine.
10. Psalm 63:1, 3, 6, 8, emphasis mine.
11. Hirsch, *Redeeming Sex*, 26.
12. Hirsch, *Redeeming Sex*, 26.
13. C. S. Lewis references this in his infamous essay "The Harem Within" when he says, "After all, almost the main work of life is to come out of our selves, out of the little, dark prison we are all born in." C. S. Lewis, *The Collected Letters of C. S. Lewis*, vol. 3, *Narnia, Cambridge, and Joy, 1950–1953* (New York: HarperCollins, 2007), 758–59.
14. Rob Bell, *Sex God: Exploring the Endless Connections between Sexuality and Spirituality* (Grand Rapids: Zondervan, 2007), xiv.

Chapter 10: Turned On

1. John 2:1–11.
2. Ecclesiastes 8:15.
3. Jon Tyson, *The Burden Is Light: Liberating Your Life from the Tyranny of Performance and Success* (New York: Multnomah, 2018), 136.
4. Matthew 12:34; Proverbs 4:23; 10:11.
5. Ashley Anderson, "Disruptive Discipleship: The Pure in Heart," *Church of the City New York*, podcast, November 2, 2020.
6. Hebrews 4:15.
7. Mark Batterson, *The Circle Maker: Praying Circles around Your Biggest Dreams and Greatest Fears* (Grand Rapids: Zondervan, 2011), 15.
8. Daniel 3:17–18; Ephesians 3:20–21; James 1:17.
9. Psalm 100:4.
10. Genesis 2:18.
11. Psalm 139:4.
12. "The Happy Hour #177: Kat Harris," January 24, 2018, *The Happy Hour with Jamie Ivey*, podcast, https://jamieivey.com/17043-2/.

Chapter 11: Sexual Healing

1. "You Are Worthy of Great Sex (and So Much More): Dr. Celeste Holbrook," May 28, 2019, *For the Love with Jen Hatmaker*, podcast, 41:10–41:46, https://jenhatmaker.com/podcast/series-17/you-are-worthy-of-great-sex-and-so-much-more-dr-celeste-holbrook/.
2. Matthew 22:37.
3. Psalm 139:1.

Chapter 12: My Dirty Little Secret

1. 1 Corinthians 7:9.
2. Matthew 14:22–33.
3. Kevan Lee, "Your Brain on Dopamine: The Science of Motivation," *I Done This* (blog), April 9, 2019, http://blog.idonethis.com/the-science-of-motivation-your-brain-on-dopamine/.
4. Katherine Wu, "Love, Actually: The Science behind Lust, Attraction, and Companionship," Harvard University, February 14, 2017, http://sitn.hms.harvard.edu/flash/2017/love-actually-science-behind-lust-attraction-companionship/.
5. Donna Murray, "Oxytocin and Breastfeeding: The Hormone Responsible for Love, Bonding, and Let-Down," Very Well Family, July 15, 2019, https://www.verywellfamily.com/oxytocin-and-breastfeeding-3574977.
6. Helen Fisher, "This Is Your Brain on Sex," *On Being* with Krista Tippett, April 5, 2018, https://onbeing.org/programs/this-is-your-brain-on-sex-apr2018/. Helen Fisher, "Why We Love, Why We Cheat," TED, February 2006, https://www.ted.com/talks/helen_fisher_tells_us_why_we_love_cheat/transcript?language=en; Helen Fisher, "Helen Fisher Explains Why Casual Sex Doesn't Exist," Big Think, April 23, 2012, YouTube video, 2:10, https://www.youtube.com/watch?v=6wT61wsgfk0.
7. "How Porn Affects the Brain Like a Drug," Fight the New Drug, August 23, 2017, https://fightthenewdrug.org/how-porn-affects-the-brain-like-a-drug/.
8. I could write an entire book about how unbelievably damaging porn is, not to mention that the porn industry is inextricably

linked to sex trafficking. One of my favorite resources on pornography, and where a lot of the information for this chapter came from, is the website Fight the New Drug. One study on this particular website informs us that over 60 percent of underage sex trafficking victims say their sexual acts have been advertised and sold. "By the Numbers: Is The Porn Industry Connected to Sex Trafficking?," Fight the New Drug, July 29, 2019, https://fightthenewdrug.org/by-the-numbers-porn-sex-trafficking-connected/. Another great resource that shows us it's hardly possible to interact with porn without aiding the sex trafficking industry comes from Thorn.org. Dr. Vanessa Bouché, "A Report on the Use of Technology to Recruit, Groom and Sell Domestic Minor Sex Trafficking Victims," Thorn: Digital Defender of Children, January 2015, https://www.thorn.org/wp-content/uploads/2015/02/Survivor_Survey_r5.pdf.

9. C. S. Lewis, personal letter from Lewis to Keith Masson found in *The Collected Letters of C. S. Lewis*, vol. 3, *Narnia, Cambridge, and Joy 1950–1963* (New York: HarperCollins, 2007), 758–59.
10. *Sex in the City*, season 1, episode 9, "The Turtle and the Hare," directed by Michael Fields, written by Nicole Avril and Sue Kolinsky, aired August 2, 1998, HBO.
11. Proverbs 27:17.
12. Mark 12:29–30.
13. 1 Corinthians 6:12–13 ESV.
14. 1 Corinthians 10:23.
15. Donald Miller, *A Million Miles in a Thousand Years: What I Learned While Editing My Life* (Nashville: Thomas Nelson, 2009), 86.
16. Mark 10:14.

Chapter 13: Let's Talk about Sex

1. Genesis 2:18.
2. Genesis 2:21–22; Genesis 1:31.
3. Genesis 2:23 ESV.
4. Genesis 2:24–25 ESV.
5. Genesis 2:24.

6. Matthew Henry, *Matthew Henry's Commentary*, vol. 3 (Peabody, MA: Hendrickson, 1991), quoted in Chris Priestley, "Who Should Study Song of Solomon?," Crossroads Church, September 11, 2014, http://www.wvcrossroads.com/who-should-study-song-of-solomon/.
7. Song of Solomon 1:2. http://www.wvcrossroads.com/who-should-study-song-of-solomon/.
8. Song of Solomon 1:13.
9. Song of Solomon 4:6, 11.
10. Song of Solomon 1:2.
11. Song of Solomon 4:16.
12. Song of Solomon 5:1.
13. Song of Solomon 4:9–10.
14. Song of Solomon 5:1.
15. Song of Solomon 2:7; 3:5; 8:4 WEB.
16. Song of Solomon 4:1–8.
17. Matthew 10:30; Luke 12:7; Psalm 139:4.
18. Genesis 18:19.
19. Genesis 4:1.
20. Debra Hirsch, *Redeeming Sex: Naked Conversations about Sexuality and Spirituality* (Downers Grove, IL: InterVarsity Press, 2015), 27.
21. Genesis 2:25.
22. Christopher West, *Theology of the Body for Beginners: Rediscovering the Meaning of Life, Love, Sex, and Gender* (North Palm Beach: Wellspring, 2004), 23.
23. 1 John 4:10.
24. 1 Corinthians 6:18; 1 Corinthians 7:1-2; Ephesians 5:3 KJV.
25. Peggy Orenstein, *Girls and Sex: Navigating the Complicated New Landscape* (New York: HarperCollins, 2016), 93, 101.
26. DeVon Franklin and Meagan Good with Tim Vandehey, *The Wait: A Powerful Practice for Finding the Love of Your Life and the Life You Love* (New York: Howard, 2016), xviii.
27. Franklin, Good, and Vandehey, *The Wait*, 17.

Chapter 14: Stop Shoulding All over Yourself

1. Simon Sinek, "How Great Leaders Inspire Action," TED, September 2009, www.ted.com/talks/simon_sinek_how_great_leaders_inspire_action?language=en.

2. Ashley Abercrombie, *Rise of the Truth Teller: Own Your Story, Tell It Like It Is, and Live with Holy Gumption* (Grand Rapids: Baker, 2019), 75.
3. Sue Edwards, Kelley Matthews, and Henry Rogers, *Mixed Ministry: Working Together as Brothers and Sisters in an Oversexed Society* (Grand Rapids: Kregel, 2008), 177.
4. 1 Corinthians 6:19.
5. Rob Bell, *Sex God: Exploring the Endless Connections between Sexuality and Spirituality* (New York: Zondervan, 2007), 41.
6. 1 Corinthians 10:23.
7. Galatians 6:4–5.

Chapter 15: Blurred Lines

1. Peggy Orenstein, *Girls and Sex: Navigating the Complicated New Landscape* (New York: HarperCollins, 2016), 93.
2. The full quote is this: "Male pledgers are four times more likely to have anal sex than other young people, and pledgers of both sexes are six times more likely to engage in oral sex. What's more, by age eighteen, their resolve begins to crack; by their twenties, over 80 percent of pledgers either deny or have forgotten that they ever pledged at all. The only lesson that sticks is that they remain less likely to use contraception and drastically less likely to protect against disease. . . . Pledgers have the same rate of STDs and pregnancy as the general population, even though they begin intercourse later and report fewer sexual partners overall." Orenstein, *Girls and Sex*, 89, 255–56.
3. Michael Castleman, "The Most Important Sexual Statistic: Intercourse Is Not the Key to Most Women's Sexual Satisfaction," *Psychology Today*, March 16, 2009, https://www.psychologytoday.com/us/blog/all-about-sex/200903/the-most-important-sexual-statistic.
4. Daniel Oberhaus, "The Biggest-Ever Orgasm Study about How Women Come: The World Needs This Right Now," Vice.com, September 6, 2017, https://www.vice.com/en/article/neepb8/the-science-of-female-pleasure-still-needs-more-attention.

5. Sex as a "pool of experiences" references Professor Daniel Fortenberry's perspective. Orenstein, *Girls and Sex*, 93, 101.
6. Luke 23:43.

Chapter 16: Work on Your Ish

1. Esther 4:14 ESV.
2. Romans 8:37.
3. Bessel van der Kolk, *The Body Keeps the Score: Brain, Mind, and Body in the Healing of Trauma* (New York: Penguin, 2014), 285.

Chapter 17: The One That Got Away

1. 2 Corinthians 10:5.
2. Romans 12:2.
3. Philippians 4:8 ESV, emphasis mine.
4. Romans 8:31.
5. Ruthie Lindsey, *There I Am: The Journey from Hopelessness to Healing—A Memoir* (New York: Gallery, 2020), 212.

Chapter 18: Dating Is a Curb, Not a Cliff

1. Aziz Ansari and Eric Klinenberg, *Modern Romance* (New York: Penguin, 2015), 83.
2. C. S. Lewis, *The Four Loves* (New York: HarperCollins, 1960), 155–56.
3. Romans 5:5.

Chapter 19: Now What?

1. Ephesians 3:20–21.
2. Jen Hatmaker, *Fierce, Free, and Full of Fire: The Guide to Being Glorious You* (New York: HarperCollins, 2020), xiv.
3. Jon Tyson, "Church in a Time of Crisis: Faithfulness in a Time Compromise," *Church of the City New York*, podcast, May 11, 2020.
4. Shauna Niequist, *Cold Tangerines: Celebrating the Extraordinary Nature of Everyday Life* (Grand Rapids: Zondervan, 2007), 29.